Frustrations of a Sceptic

March 2020 – March 2021

By

Jonny Peppiatt

for all the lonely people

Foreword

The twelve months from 19th March 2020 saw the collapse of sanity, the war against science, (which, unfortunately, science lost), the loss of my life in London, the loss of friends over the war on science, and the most severe depression I'd experienced since my school years.

It also, to be fair, saw a return to cricket in a big way – even if that was then subsequently taken away again, a promotion, the completion of my ACA qualification, the publication of my second novel, *Frayed Edges*, a deepening of familial bonds, *Regular Contributor* status with *Lockdown Sceptics*, and an extensive amount of writing.

So, while it was a time that I am sure will go down in history as one of the greatest atrocities against humanity, I must admit that, once I had bounced back from the depression, I came away largely unscathed.

When the actual pandemic began, I started a blog to discuss my learnings on depression, as well as to fill some time having been thrown into Lockdown 1. This blog is published in full in this book and makes up Part One, *An Unprecedented Time*.

As I wrote this blog, my feelings on the Lockdown were largely neutral. We were told that this was a once in a century killer virus, I trusted our Government, I trusted the BBC, and I was, to my shame, worried about the virus.

More than this though, I was busy with work. I didn't have the spare time that was needed to think for myself, or to do the research and find the information that was out there on why the Lockdowns were such a catastrophically bad idea.

Nor did I have the inclination or justification to question what we were being told by what turned out to be one of the most corrupt Governments in history and the spineless mainstream media.

I still didn't have the time when I commenced the writing of a series for work which sought to cover the range of social causes of depression and anxiety. This series is published in full in Part Two, *Notes to Work*.

It was once this series was written, in the summer, (the dates under the titles of that series reference the date each article was sent to my colleagues, not the date of writing), that I switched to part-time working and began to really commit myself to finding out what the Government and the BBC weren't telling us.

My focus from early September became almost exclusively on combatting the lockdowns in whatever way I could.

This almost exclusively came in the form of writing articles or poems that voiced my concerns. However, I did also spend hours upon hours discussing the issues with quite literally whoever would listen.

These articles, poems, and other somewhat sillier pieces are what make up the second half of this book, Part Three, *The Lockdown Files*, and I have published them here as a reminder to myself, and as proof for anyone else, that I was on what I believe will turn out to be the right side of history.

It should be noted that the pieces subtitled with "*Published in Lockdown Sceptics on...*" are my personal edits and are therefore not necessarily entirely representative of the views held by those at *Lockdown Sceptics*.

Contents

Part One – An Unprecedented Time

To kick it all off	9
A little word on maintaining our mental health right now	13
Let's talk about sport	18
A little word on words	23
Let's get hypocritical	27
The Great White Mountain	31
When the cat is hungry, he'll let you know	36
The Platitudinal *At least*	40
The Careless Colloquialisms	44
Variety is the spice of life, and unfortunately Tesco is out of stock	49
I've literally just written this because Marcus won't stop berating me for not writing more	53
A little dose of positivity	58
I actually had fun this week	63
Guilt and Mistakes	69
The End	74

Part Two – Notes to Work

Intrinsic and extrinsic motivations	81
A hopeful future	86
Status and Respect	91
Hidden pasts, shame, and grief	96
The Natural World	102
Loneliness	106
Meaningful Work	112
Measures and Mental Health	119

Part Three – The Lockdown Files

10 reasons to be anti-lockdown	126
Why is scepticism not growing?	130
It Waits for Me	134
The rise in depression is not something that will disappear when the lockdowns end	136
A postcard of "long-Covid" from my sofa	142
Questions for the PM and the Health Secretary	147
Let's turn the questions back on the lockdown proponents	150
Queer Culture	153
Let me be free	161
In what can I hope?	163
A Red-List Analysis	165
The Great Escape	171
The One Who Couldn't Actually Get Away	176
Opportunity, Incentive, and Rationalisation	179
Level of Population Immunity in the UK	187
The Launch of *Lockdown? What Lockdown?*	192
Lockdown? What Lockdown? Post One	194
Lockdown? What Lockdown? Post Two	195
Why Lockdowns don't work	197
I'm not "antivaxx", but…	202
The Great Mask Exemption Lanyard Debate	206
We Must Strive for the Return of Trust	215
Given an inch, I'm going to take a mile	220
Risk of mortality in patients infected with SARS-CoV-2 variant of concern 202012/1" matched cohort study	224
What might I have got wrong?	230

Some basic maths on the testing	237
Have Lockdowns worked in any way?	241
There'll be a day	249
Closing remarks and thanks	250

Part One

An Unprecedented Time

To kick it all off

21ˢᵗ March 2020

Thursday 19th March was by no means day 1 of what's been going on around the world, but it is where I've decided to start this account from, because that was the day that I left London. It was the day when I realised that I would be completely alone if I stayed put in SW19, and it was also the day that I'd had a single triple chocolate chip cookie for lunch for the second day running because I'd not been able to source bread or other lunchy supplies from Sainsbury's across the road, or the creativity to make lunch out of what I had, and it was also the day that the last of my commitments – and by 'commitments' I mean things to look forward to and break up the monotony that life would otherwise be simplified into offering – for the next six weeks was cancelled.

And yet, I felt no sense of fear or dread at this point. Quite on the contrary, when Guy (my brother) and I turned left to start the drive out of London down to the family home in Surrey I was overcome by a sense of bizarre novelty, the realisation that this wasn't "popping home for the night", but rather that this was fleeing for the countryside, brought a nervous laugh to the front of my mouth.

I am, undoubtably, in a fortunate position for a number of reasons: my job (and salary) is secure; I can work from home; I have a large family that I can lean on; my family home is generous with the space it offers – even with a large family; and, to pass time, I am more than happy to write. However, I also have a long history of struggling with my mental health, and because of this have spent an inordinate amount of time pondering the myriad facets of depression: how it presents itself; why it comes and goes; what triggers lapses; what it means; how it feels.

I'm sure that I will talk about many different things that I've learnt, realised, or come to believe over the coming weeks, but the point I want to start on to introduce this whatever-this-is is that depression holds no prejudices; it doesn't look at your family, your upbringing, your financial security, your 'privilege', or anything else. It strikes wherever and whenever it wants. It is true that most people will be started on their journey of living with a depression that strikes wherever and whenever because of a time that either steadily worked them down to a desperately dark place, or that bought them a ticket for the bullet train, packed their bags, and then burned their luggage and strapped them to the front of the train just as it set off, but once you've hit that low once, two things become very difficult: getting out for the first time; and staying out from then on.

This is why I decided to start writing this, because after Thursday evening's sense of novelty and nervous excitement, it took as little as twenty-four hours to drop to a place where I was in an endless almost pitch-black tunnel where the only visible light was that bullet train coming back for round two.

What exactly happened during that very short time to bring about that drastic change in attitude? I worked from home, as I had been all week; the pubs that I'd been avoiding all week shut; the cricket season that I'd been expecting to be cancelled altogether was only cancelled up to May 28th meaning that only three of my forty-two planned sporting spectating events were cancelled; and I had dinner with my mum and brothers. On balance, nothing in there made my situation any worse – if anything it was a series of events to not even be indifferent about, but to be cautiously optimistic about.

And this is the now probably fairly predictable point, it didn't matter.

I've called this "An unprecedented time" because that is what everyone keeps saying, and it certainly is, but what is not even remotely unprecedented is that life is often a struggle and, even when it isn't, our emotions can turn in the blink of an eye and make what is already a bit of a struggle close to unbearable. On that note though, what is very much unprecedented in our lifetime is having the entire world struggling because of the same thing, and it's because of this that I sat down and opened up Word this morning.

Yes, I am writing this because it is one way that I know I can stop myself from walking back into that tunnel; yes, I am writing this because it's also a way I know I can find the door out of that tunnel if I find myself wandering into it; but I am also writing it because there is a chance that reading it might help someone else stay on relatively happy path.

My plan is to talk about three things as the entries accumulate here: what I have discovered from my experiences with depression; what I am doing to look after myself in these 'unprecedented times'; and anything I think might help you or anyone else with looking after yourself at the same time. And with that, I'm going to sign off now and go have a knock-about outside with my cousin to get some exercise and fresh air, because, although emotionally this is a dark and frightening time, the sun is actually shining this morning, and I need to take the little wins where I can.

Stay happy and stay you.

A little word on maintaining our mental health right now

22nd March 2020

With so many people working from home, or just stuck at home, now more than ever we need to spend some time thinking about how we can look after our mental health, because this is unquestionably a time of stress and anxiety, and while I'm sure we all appreciate the severity of the physical side of what is happening worldwide, those who suffer from anxiety, depression, or compulsion disorders will certainly be struggling acutely at this time, and even for those without diagnosed disorders, the next few days/weeks/maybe even months will be challenging.

With regards to compulsion disorders, the invaluable advice you will have heard every day is to wash your hands regularly for at least twenty seconds. This is seemingly crucial advice in slowing the spread, but we also need to be conscious that we are following this advice 'regularly', and not excessively. Now that we are working from home, it is easier to take note of what is excessive: if you have not gone out during the day, there is no need to be washing your hands more than you should on a typical day, that being after visiting the bathroom, and before cooking or eating.

With regards to anxiety, the world is talking about this pandemic, every minute of every day right now, and that is a huge amount of nearly unavoidable information. If you want to watch the news, it's there;

if you want to catch up on sport (or on what sport has been cancelled), it's there; if you want to scroll through your socials, it's there; if you want to read my blog, it's here. This amount of inundation can be damaging, and if you are finding that it is causing you stress, the advice coming out of the WHO is to set aside time to catch up on the news only once or twice a day, and that you use this time specifically to inform yourself with practical advice for making plans and decisions going forward.

With regards to depression, there are two pieces of advice that I believe are important and worth sharing. The first considers routines. Life in its current form will most likely throw your routines into chaos; be conscious of this, set aside some time to think about how you can establish new routines, and then stick to these.

For example, you may be taking advantage of the additional hour in bed in the morning that you can now afford due to commuting time being cut, or you may be going to bed an hour later knowing that you have this additional time in the morning. While this may seem appealing, especially as getting additional sleep will both help us avoid burnout and will boost our immune systems in a time when that is vitally important, we are creatures of habit, and deviating from our routines can be discombobulating. Consider instead the possibility of going to bed an hour earlier than usual and then getting up at your usual time and fitting something into that new morning slot such as meditation, or some exercise; although, I do appreciate that exercise will be a difficult one right now with 5-a-side leagues, indoor leagues, gyms, etc. all closed and cancelled, but there is a whole world of exercise programs designed for people who only have access to their living rooms or a small garden, including apps like Freeletics, the NHS website, or even the depths of your own creativity.

The second piece of advice considers connections. Again, this is a difficult one given that people are either self-isolating, or social distancing, but this is by no means impossible. Everyone has at some point experienced loneliness to one degree or another at one time or another, but this is going to be a time when vast swathes of people are suffering simultaneously. The only benefit to this is that, if you are feeling lonely, you will hopefully not experience the typically coexistent feeling of being weak and the belief that your loneliness is unjustified, and this means that it should be easier to put in the effort to stay connected.

If your job involves working in a team, then ensure that you are having regular catch-ups, ensure that juniors have been properly coached on what they are expected to do, and maybe even set aside some time where the team can all be on a call together, not to discuss anything in particular, but to use this time to ask questions, tell stories, chat, simply communicate as if you were all in the room together.

Regarding the personal side of connections, the exact same advice applies: have regular catch-ups with friends and family; check in with people you know may be struggling to make sure they have everything they need; or set up group video calls. One option you have during the working day though is to time and synchronise your coffee breaks with a friend so that you can call them up and have that five/ten-minute chat about whatever it is that you would normally talk about in the break-out area or kitchen at your office.

The advice you'll have heard coming out of the Government has been to keep the elderly in mind, to call and chat and give them some company, but be sure to also keep in mind anyone you know who lives alone, or who you know doesn't get on with their housemates, or who is starting to feel overwhelmed by the constant family company, and will be feeling the pinch of loneliness particularly hard right now.

Always remember that we are social creatures, and this means that if you are feeling like you really want to talk to someone, there will be plenty of people in your contacts who are feeling exactly the same; you'd be amazed what a difference it will make to someone's day to receive an apparently random call where you check up on how they're getting on – even if you're only really calling because you're going stir crazy yourself!

This is a worrying time of social distancing, and keeping apart, yes, but this also means that it is exactly the time when we need to pull together, albeit needing to be slightly creative about how we pull together.

Stay happy and stay you.

Let's talk about sport

23rd March 2020

"Of course, there are more important things right now." – [insert name of anyone talking about sport on the news right now]

I'm not disagreeing, [insert name of anyone talking about sport on the news right now] is right, there are more important things right now, but just because something isn't the most important thing right now, doesn't mean it isn't worth talking about. One reason I want to talk about sport is because I've noticed over recent times that I've often censored myself to not talk about sport. Now, most of you reading this will be shocked by that last statement because it simply won't ring true, and some of you will even be trying – and struggling – to remember the last conversation we had where I didn't bring up cricket, but if that is the case, then it means you haven't been a part of my "private life".

Unless, that is, you're the guy who cited me being "too obsessed with cricket" as one of the reasons for calling it quits on what I later realised was just a terrible fit that was doomed from the start, not least because there is no such thing as "too obsessed with cricket". What utter nonsense. "Cricket is life" after all, and how could one be too obsessed with life?

What's particularly odd about this self-censorship within my private life and when I'm around the gay community though is that it's a bizarre mirror image of the way that I felt "encouraged" to get more invested in and knowledgeable about sport so that I could appear "less gay" at school. Again, what utter nonsense. But, however nonsensical the intention, I was steadily saturated with a love of sport that has stayed with me to this day.

Over the years, however, as I learnt to look after my skin, pluck, and do a light layer of make-up, as RuPaul's drag race and queer eye became staples in my TV diet, and as the frequency of my visits to Heaven and other specifically gay (and yet welcoming of all) establishments became the only nights out that I would go on, I didn't find myself getting any "more gay", (in part, I'm sure, because by this point I'd realised that what someone does and how they act defining your sexuality is a ridiculous notion), I just found the divide between the version of me that won't shut up about cricket and the version of me that wears make-up getting wider.

Let me be clear before this starts to sound like I've developed a case of split personality disorder; I don't see this wide divide, and that there are two distinct versions of me, as a problem, even in the slightest. We show slight variants of ourselves to each different person or in each different social setting that we find ourselves in, and that is okay, because it is the sum of these variations that make up who we are.

To highlight this, imagine me strutting into a training session on a Sunday morning wearing skinny jeans, the what-is-now-a-little-too-form-fitting t-shirt printed with a rainbow design that spells out "Straight outta the closet", make-up on, and a silver floral earing in the piercing I got when I heard the saying "right ear, right queer". It's not an ideal fit. The point here is that those I socialise with on a Friday evening typically don't want to hear about cricket, and those who I socialise with on a Sunday morning typically don't want to hear about RuPaul, but at different times, I want to talk about both, and now, by having these different social settings, I can do that; by having these different social settings, I can add them together and be myself, completely.

Of course, these are just two sides among many others, such as who I am at work, or with my family, or with my cat (that can be a weird one), or even on my own (this is definitely the weirdest one – thank god none of you have, or ever will, know that side). And, finally, at the ripe old age of twenty-four, I can say with absolute (about 49%) certainty, that I have reached the pinnacle of my growth and development.

Okay, I accept that I will continue to change and be moulded by events that happen to me and around me, but, where I am now, I feel that all my sides connect and allow me to be a complete version of myself, and it's a version that I love, which is, of course, the most important thing here, and not just because "If you don't love yourself, how the hell you gonna love somebody else?" – RuPaul Charles.

But this is exactly why we need to talk about sport, or, as you may have realised, anything that you normally do on a weekly/daily/hourly basis that has been taken away from you because of the restrictions we are currently facing. Yes, there are more important things right now than sport, I agree. But sport is something that millions upon millions (including myself) have built one of their "sides" upon, and if you were only a triangle before these restrictions came in, you're now stuck being nothing more than a pair of floating lines awkwardly hinged at one end.

I said earlier that we each show a different side of ourselves depending on the social setting we find ourselves in. Well, if we're all in Lockdown to some degree or another, then the chances are that we are going to find ourselves stuck on one side, and that has the potential to be unbelievably frustrating for ourselves, not just because it'll become repetitive and dull, but because we are all a magnificent variety of shapes, and being asked to be a line day after day could eradicate any sense of completeness that you have within yourself.

Yesterday I said that we needed to be creative with how we pull together; today I'm going to suggest that we be open to being creatively supportive and that we be open with others about how they can support you. If you find yourself feeling incomplete and like you're missing a side of yourself, experiment with bringing that side out to whomever you're in lockdown with, because that could be fun for everyone. Or, alternatively, explain how much this side of you means to you, maybe forward them this blog, and then find a way of including them in this part of your life – you will only end up closer for it.

Stay happy and, most relevant to today's post, stay you.

A little word on words

24th March 2020

It may be entirely apparent from everything that I've either written or said to you that I am a huge fan of words, both in the sense that you can play with them to create language art in the form of striking sentences that roll off the tongue in such a way that they can only be described as tasty, and also in the way that you can put simple sounds together to do anything from convey information, to express thoughts that have sprung from the depths of your imagination, or to evoke significant emotional reactions.

A lot of you, if not all of you will have seen the chart that says that 55% of our communication is non-verbal (eye-contact, body language, facial expressions and so on), while our words only account for 7%.

When I first saw this chart, I fundamentally disagreed with it, because I rashly inferred that it was saying our words barely mattered; however, with a little more thought, as is often the case, I realised I was wrong and that this wasn't what it was saying at all, rather it was saying that if we are not careful with the words we choose, there's a very good chance they will be misunderstood.

The point here is that our words hold within in them the possibility of being both incredibly useful and potently powerful, and, as such, they need to be treated with boundless respect. And this is what I want to discuss today, not least because in a lot of cases now we will have lost that 55% above, but also because our words do matter and they do have impact.

It doesn't take much reflection to know how true this statement is, all you need to do is think back to an occasion when you felt like you weren't entirely yourself and someone said something to you that let you know that they cared; maybe they told you that they were there for you, maybe they said that they hoped you were okay, or maybe they even said the words "I care".

On the other hand, maybe they didn't say any of this, or, more likely, maybe you didn't hear them say any of this.

The difficulty that we need to be mindful of is that everything we say always has two meanings: what we intend our words to mean, and what our words are perceived to mean. How often have you opened up to someone about something you're going through and the response you receive is for this person to start telling you about a time when they went through something they believe to be vaguely and yet sufficiently similar that it is worth telling you about?

While this may come across as insensitive self-absorption, this is much more likely just their way of saying "I empathise, I understand what you're going through, you can trust me, I want to help however I can. I care." But this can be near impossible to appreciate when you're trying to talk about your problem and all that you can hear from your confidante is them talking about their problem.

So, what does this mean for us in our day to day lives? Well, quite a lot to be honest, but most importantly it means that when we choose our words, we need to be conscious of the potential perceptions people could have of them because if we understand how they can be misunderstood then we can do more to avoid that happening. A person can only see through their own eyes after all, and everything they see, or hear, will be tinted by their experiences.

It also means that we need to ensure that what we are saying gets us as close to the meaning that we are intending will be perceived; it means that when we are being spoken to, we need to really listen for the intended meaning and not default to our own perceived meanings; and, finally, it means that we should trust in the good in people and strive to assume that the intended meaning is the best possible meaning.

We are undoubtably living in strange and frightening times right now, where much of our communication is happening electronically, a method which often loses the emotional nuances, but, even so, I have been quite moved by the regularity with which people have checked in and let me know that they care, and I hope that is the same for everyone.

All I can say now is keep checking in with people, keep telling and showing people you care, keep looking after yourselves and one another, and remember, as we head into another day of lockdown, that you can make a difference with only your words.

Stay happy and stay you.

Let's get hypocritical

25th March 2020

I realised a couple of nights ago as Alice and I settled down to a bit of TV at about half past midnight that I wasn't doing particularly well at following my own advice of maintaining a routine or even going to bed a little bit earlier than usual.

This realisation came just after I'd abandoned the idea of doing a post about making sure we treat our worries in a healthy self-medicating way, namely by not drinking too much. I abandoned this idea in part because I didn't think I could stretch that out to a full post, in part because it came with too great a risk of sounding judgemental, and in part because Al, Pa, and I had just polished off our third bottle of wine since sitting down for dinner.

Then again, one of the biggest reasons that I'm writing this blog is to help me look out for myself, and if I think I should probably be tempering my alcohol intake, or that I need to think about my routines again, then I probably should pop it in here, if only to remind myself.

Al and I were sat outside yesterday, basking in the final throws of the sun, discussing this blog, and she made the comment that a lot of what I say is simple, obvious, and common, but that the thoughts I write would not come to her formally structured, so to see them written down gives her a sense of connection and validation. The valuable point here is that all of us, me included, often know what is good for us and how to look after ourselves, but, despite this, we then find a way to stumble and fall short of the bar that we set for ourselves.

Is it disappointing when we stay up too late when we know we have work in the morning, or when we have a couple more glasses of wine than we know we should, or we put off kicking the ciggies to the kerb for another day, or we say something that upsets or annoys someone we care about? Yes, of course it can be. But let's not be too hard on ourselves; the very fact that it's disappointing shows that you're trying to do better, and for that, I say well done you, keep going champ.

The point is, it isn't a sign of weakness to offer up advice and then have the simultaneity of your failure to adhere to this offered up advice slap you in the face, so long as you're trying, because continuing to try in the face of failure is often the greatest sign of strength.

The other thing that I wanted to talk about today, which will lead nicely into another piece of slightly hypocritical advice as you sit there reading my blog on your phone, is technology. Long before we were all put on lockdown, you may remember that we talked about lots of things that weren't pandemic, and one of those things was excessive digital content, social media, and screen time.

Right now, as I write this, I have spent most of the day at my laptop for work, with both my personal phone and my work phone either next to me or in my hand, and, now, with face-to-face communication with those outside of your household gone (bar FaceTime and the like), this has become not just normal, but necessary.

We need, and want, to stay in contact, and so the number of emails, calls, messages, etc. that we send and that have come through has risen significantly lately, and then, because we can't go out, when we want to pass some mindless time, we use our phones for entertainment; when we want to check the news, we use our phones; when we want to read my blog, we use our phones.

Of course, you may already be finding time to read, or do some gardening, or going out for your one run a day; but, if not, these are great ideas, because being constantly logged on, constantly contactable, constantly drip-fed the news could compound your stress in what is already a stressful time.

To pull together two pieces of advice from previous posts, and to ensure it doesn't sound like I'm contradicting myself, I'm going to suggest, as I said yesterday, that we make sure we have some time to check in with friends and family; as mentioned a few days ago, we set aside a specific time to keep informed on the current status of our situation, thus limiting the endless supply of worrisome and anxiety-inducing news; and, to wrap up today, that we also set aside some time to digitally distance, if for no other reason than to give your mind a chance to declutter itself and to give you a chance to look after yourself.

It is amazing the amount that we are checking in with others and making sure that everyone we know and care about is okay, but it is also important to remember to take time for you, check in with you, and spend some time really making sure that you are okay.

Stay happy and stay you.

P.S. Tomorrow I will be digitally distancing. See you Friday.

The Great White Mountain

27th March 2020

Dr. Alvaro Pascual-Leone came up with the metaphor that our brains are like a snowy hill and our thoughts are sleds upon that hill, working their way from the top to the bottom, and I'm going to use a variation of this metaphor an excessive amount today.

Right at the start of this blog I said that I would use this space to talk about what I've learned from my experiences with depression, both my own experiences and my interaction with those close to me who have suffered, and this is going to be my focus today. I am going to take this metaphor of the snowy hill, edit it just a touch, and then use it to explain a few things about depression that are crucial to really understanding what it is.

So, first, the edit: this snowy hill is now a whole mountain, because we're wonderful complex creatures, and I don't think likening our brains to a hill does them justice when we can have a whole mountain; and the sleds are now skiers, in part because I think it's easier to think about the motion of a skier, but mainly because I'm still bummed out that Avoriaz shut before we could go this year.

Now, thinking about this mountain, consider certain factors such as the gradient of the slope, the space available, the depth of the snow, and so on; these are all uncontrollable, and as such can be likened to our genes, or our upbringing. Other variables such as the speed at which we attack the slope, the turns we make, the time we take to stop, pick up the rocks, and throw them to the side, these are up to us.

In nature, everything follows the path of least resistance, and our thoughts are no different. When we're born, the mountain has a fresh covering of snow and no pistes to note, and a skier may take whatever path they choose, but, over time, we establish routes, lifts, bars and restaurants, entire resorts and towns, and in doing so, the way in which we think becomes rooted within us.

The first thing that becomes blindingly obvious at this point is that every single person's way of thinking is going to be slightly different because not only was the shape of each person's mountain going to be different at the beginning, but their piste maps are all going to be different as well, and having an appreciation of this fact can significantly improve our ability to be empathetic and caring of others.

The second point that becomes easy to make refers us back to the point I made on Wednesday that we need to regularly check in with ourselves. Think of this as clearing the rocks from the pistes: if we don't, then over time, skiing these routes will become fraught with danger, and the enjoyment we would typically derive from flying down the mountain steadily gets replaced with stress.

Depression is what happens when these rocks are allowed to build up to the point that the route becomes impassable and the skiers are forced to either take off their skis and walk – which is a monumental effort – or to create new paths. Often what happens as these new paths are established though is that they end up leading to a place where the only option is to take a lift back to where you started and then ski that path again, and again.

And these paths, the only paths that you've been left to take, and the paths that you are now repeatedly taking, are thoughts that you wouldn't normally have, but thoughts that are now on such a regular loop that you come to believe that not only are they true, but that there are no other possibilities.

This is the chattering voice that constantly tells you that the once pristine pistes that are now littered with rocks are not worth clearing, and it's the persistent repetitive loop that says no one will want to help you clear the piste, and if you won't do it, and no one else will do it, there is no possibility that the piste will ever be cleared again. This is who you are now. This is your life now.

The cognitive behavioural therapy that I did after what is still to this day my last depression in the latter half of 2015 focussed on three things: finding ways of quickly identifying the rocks on my pistes; finding ways of reminding myself that there are people around me who will always want to help me clear these rocks when I ask; and finding ways to help me clear these rocks myself.

Everything I have said to you in the previous five posts has in some way stemmed from one of these three things. By maintaining connections, we can consistently remind ourselves that there are people who care, people around us who will help us move rocks should we ask them; by being true to ourselves and being open about who we are with those around us, we can keep a clear picture of who we are and therefore always be confident in the knowledge of our piste maps and avoid getting lost through the woods, stuck on one of those endless loops; by checking in with other people, we can show them that we care, letting them know that we will move every single rock we can for them; and by allowing time to check in with ourselves we can keep an eye on those rocks, and always be aware whenever a new one pops up.

Depression is unfortunately so common and yet so misunderstood, and so I'd just like to leave you with a final few thoughts. First, if someone you know and care about is suffering, don't put it on yourself to be the one who needs to fix them, that is a level of responsibility that will only bring you down; instead, appreciate that they are either putting in an amount of effort comparable to walking up and down a rocky mountain in ski boots with their skis in their arms just to think straight, or that they are not thinking in the same way you have come to know they think. If you truly appreciate this, then you will be one step closer to truly understanding what they are going through, and that will make a huge difference.

Second, if you constantly let them know you care, you will be doing so much, just because it has the power to show them that the voice that won't relent and is telling them that no one will help them clear the rocks might be wrong.

Finally, there's really no need to wait for a depression to come on for us to keep telling and showing those we care about just how much we care about them. Let's do it today and spend a little time keeping the pistes of our loved ones clear. And, to put that point into action, if you're reading this, you're most likely either a friend or a family member of mine, so, whether you're struggling at the moment or not, know that I care about you.

Stay happy and stay you.

When the cat is hungry, he'll let you know

29th March 2020

It's 5:30am (except, it isn't, because it's really still only 4:30) and I'm sat downstairs in the kitchen with a cigarette and a cup of chamomile tea because Shere Khan (my cat) got hungry and decided his need for food exceeded my need for sleep. This happens from time to time, especially recently because his vet told us off the other day saying that "we need to talk about his weight".

Usually it's fine, I can give him a handful of food and go straight back to sleep, but the boiler had also decided that it had had enough at some point in the night, and for a brief moment, as the tip of my nose fuzzed with a pink glow in the cold, I thought that maybe this whole pandemic nonsense wasn't happening and I was high up in the alps.

Alas, no, it's just about five degrees in my room in Surrey.

The odd part about this though, is that I'm not nearly as fussed as I think I normally would be. There's probably an element of Shere adorably climbing into bed and curling up next to me with his asshole in my face that softened the blow, but I think there are really two forces in play that are making me feel okay with it being twenty to six in the morning as I roll another ciggie and write up these thoughts.

The first is that I am very much missing my alone time, almost as much as I am missing live sport. Yes, the space we have down here in Surrey is sufficient that I could probably go an entire day without seeing anyone I'm in lockdown with if I wanted to, but there's a reason I haven't put any effort into looking for a housemate, and there is a big difference between being on your own and having some space to yourself, and I like being on my own; not for extended periods of time – I'm much happier spending the three weeks here than I would be spending it alone – but certainly for a few hours a day; enough time to introspect and keep myself grounded, but not so much that I become a cliché destined to be a starving artist with a BSc and an ACA.

So, to be downstairs in the kitchen right now, knowing that everyone is asleep, knowing that I can truly be alone without any possibility of being disturbed, well it's settling that niggling little voice that says I should run away back to Wimbledon for a few days – not that that voice is particularly audible over the volume of Guy's personality.

Just joking, you know you bring me so much joy.

The second reason I'm okay with the cat's arse and the near on freezing temperature waking me up is because I feel that the typically British need to lightly bemoan one's situation has somehow faded. Now, of course, as the sun slips from view for the next few days, I'm sure we'll pick this up again to some degree – because there is little we do that is more British than to keep calm and carry on moaning about the weather, but it has struck me how infrequently, if at all, people are complaining about the abnormality and inconvenience of what life is right now.

Perhaps a part of this is because most of our complaining is a light-hearted, and yet also somewhat perverted form of one-upmanship, so, now, with everyone in the same boat, there's really no point to it, but I think it's more that there is a powerful and positive sense of the collective in play, with the primary focus being on making sure everyone else is okay and coping, on finding a way in which we can do our part, and on looking out for one another.

I had considered doing a post that highlighted some of the uplifting stories coming out of this mess, but this is what is underpinning all those uplifting stories: a shift in the inherent nature of people away from egocentricity.

Now, don't misunderstand me, while I am so heartened with the positive attitudes I am seeing both around me, and on the news around the world, if you are struggling and do need to reach out to someone, even if it is just for a rant or a moan, you should definitely do this. What all of this is saying is that you will have plenty of people who will be more than happy to listen and help you in whatever way they can.

The final piece of advice I will offer up this morning before I head back to bed is that you do make time for yourself as well, even if it is just an hour in the morning before anyone else in lockdown with you wakes up. Of course, if you don't have a cat's bottom to get you up, and you don't fancy setting an alarm for 5am – what sane person (other than my amazing mother) would – then set aside some time in the day and tell those in your household that you would appreciate not being disturbed. They will understand, they will want to help, and, if you want some time for introspection, it's likely they will too, and this will mean, therefore, that they will also almost certainly be grateful.

Stay happy and stay you.

The Platitudinal *At least*

30th March 2020

You will all have seen the news surrounding the near on unbelievable numbers of people stepping up and volunteering to help the NHS over the coming weeks, and, if this shows anything, it is that we have an inbuilt desire to look out for others. Or that we've been put in lockdown and get bored easily. But let's assume the former and hope it doesn't make an ass out of you and me.

I thought, therefore, that I would spend a little time looking at how we go about looking after each other, thinking about what's helpful, and what could be not only unhelpful, but also damaging, because, however good our intentions, we have all found ourselves in situations where we've tried to be helpful and supportive and just ended up saying something that makes it all worse.

The first thing I'll say is that we should never underestimate the power of silence. So many of us have found ourselves in situations where someone has reached out and where we then feel the need to try and fill perfectly good comfortable silences with words of support even though the very fact that you are present can be more impactful than any words out there.

But, I really want to look at two specific (and related) examples of where we can easily misstep in the context of a depression. The first arises from the fact that, when in a depression, it becomes very difficult to contextualise and this means that what would normally either go unnoticed or would present itself as only a mild inconvenience can end up feeling like an insurmountable problem that is draining the air out of you. Understanding that someone's pain is both subjective and relative can go a long way to guiding us in the way we help those around us who are struggling.

While it may seem like pointing out that this problem shouldn't be a problem, or that it "isn't that bad" could help someone contextualise, it can often have the opposite effect and make the person you're trying to help feel worse about themselves because all they've heard is someone pointing out that they've failed to assess a situation.

It will also be invaluable in our mission to look out for others to understand that those with depression are often just as clueless as you are when it comes to identifying reasons for why they feel the way they do. Of course, though, when you mix a depression with the lack of a justification you often create a crippling dose of guilt that then wraps itself around them and their depression with a vicelike grip, meaning that any comment suggesting something "isn't that bad" just exacerbates the guilt and strengthens its grip.

The other tactic that is often employed in attempts to be helpful is to highlight comparatives with the platitudinal At least. The reason I want to mention this is because it is less obvious that this is just as bad as "isn't that bad"; perhaps, because it's so much more common to throw in a throw away "at least you're not [insert anything; it makes no difference]" we forget to think about what it is we're actually saying, because, realistically, this is just a more specific example of the "isn't that bad" comment. With the platitudinal at least, instead of saying "your feelings are unjustified", it's saying "this is what would justify your feelings".

Yes, there are times when letting someone know that they're blowing something out of proportion can help them gain some perspective and get some chill, but can you be sure they're not suffering from something more serious, especially if being overwhelmed by the "little things" is such a tell-tale sign for something more serious?

It was encouraging to see that an additional £5m of funding has been provided to support mental health workers in this country, but let's not forget that we are our loved ones' front line here, so, as we continue to do what we can to support the people we care about, keep in mind that although we are all going through this together, any given person's emotions are only their own, and any given person's experience is theirs alone.

Stay happy and stay you.

The Careless Colloquialisms

2nd April 2020

Robin Skynner, known as an innovator in the field of treating mental illness, said "If people can't control their own emotions, then they have to start trying to control other people's behaviour.", and this is the somewhat negative side of the underlying sentiment present in political correctness and the 'safe space' movement.

Of course, the original idea of political correctness, an idea to which I fully subscribe, is that we should look out for those who are less capable of looking out for themselves; it's the same idea that so much of this blog has been gently suggesting. The idea that we should change our behaviour for the comfort of others, however, sounds a little Orwellian and requires a little more thought.

I have already discussed how there is a responsibility on us to listen carefully to what others say in order to be more discerning in what the intended meaning behind their words is, and the same applies here: before taking offense, it is important to appreciate whether offense was intended, and, when offense is not intended, and this is appreciated, but it is still taken nonetheless, it is then on us to control that emotional reaction and decide how we act in response.

One of the ways we can respond, of course, is to educate, because if someone has unintentionally caused offense with their words, then, by definition, they will not understand the reasons why it causes offense.

Recently, I was on a team with a couple of people that I'd never worked with before, or even met before, and, over the course of the job, they both used a phrase that made me rather uncomfortable. In part this would have been because I hadn't heard someone say "you're such a pouf" for several years and it took me by surprise and shocked me, but also because it is just a phrase that makes me uncomfortable.

One thought that came to mind since was to question if one of the reasons I hadn't heard a phrase like that for so long was simply because I haven't spent much time around people who weren't aware of my sexuality for so long, and I therefore questioned if people were still using this kind of language, only, not when they are around me. Because, if this were to be the case, it would suggest that they thought that the only time when using that sort of language wasn't okay was when they were around someone they knew to be gay.

After all, there's no link to homosexuality in the colloquial use of all these words that literally mean gay, so, what's the harm?

Hm.

There are two reasons why I find the use of these careless colloquialisms discomfiting, and neither of those is simply 'because I'm gay'.

The first is exactly because there is no link to homosexuality in the colloquial use of these words. "Gay" does not mean "gay". It means a little bit pathetic, it means a little bit limp, a little bit useless, and because it means these things, when I have to describe myself with one of these words, those are the things that it feels like I am describing myself with. That's a bummer, yes, but I can deal with it; what makes the use of this language so damaging is when younger people who have not had the confidence to 'come out' yet are faced with it and they then find themselves struggling to identify themselves in any way that does not require putting themselves down.

The second comes from the surveys that YouGov do on a yearly basis regarding LGBT issues. Currently, nearly one in three Brits still believe that being gay is a choice, and (probably the same) one in three Brits think there is something wrong with homosexuality. One in three!

Now, that doesn't mean that one in three Brits are likely to attack a gay person on a London night bus (which is still something that happens on occasion), but if I hear someone using language like "you're such a pouf", however innocently, the chances that they will fall into that one in three increase massively, because, if hearing these sorts of phrases created a very conscious link between my sexuality and believing I was therefore also synonymously "a little bit pathetic", then the likelihood is that using this language will at least create a subconscious link – even if they claim there is no link to homosexuality in the colloquial use of all these words that literally mean gay, and that is going to put me on edge around them until lengthy conversations can be had that can assure me they definitely do not fall into this population.

The other careless colloquialism I want to discuss is "that's so depressing". It is a phrase that is used often and is used to mean "this bums me out a bit". If you didn't know before, I hope that reading earlier posts in this blog have made it clear that there is a significant difference between a depression and being upset. Yes, there is a spectrum of degrees of severity of depression; yes, there is a spectrum of degrees of sadness; no, they are not the same spectrum. A prolonged feeling of deep sadness is a symptom of depression, but it is only one symptom.

By likening depression to mild sadness, as a phrase like "that's so depressing" does – however inadvertently – we can both perpetuate a deep seeded misunderstanding of the mental health disorder and belittle the fight that those who have struggled with depression have had to face. And, although my knowledge is limited in other fields of mental health, the same, I'm sure, can be said for other disorders when phrases such as "that's so OCD", or calling someone a "schizo", or "this is giving me anxiety" are used.

Yes, we have a responsibility to control our own emotions, and a responsibility to be discerning about what other people say and mean, but we also have a responsibility to think about the wider ramifications that our own words can have, regardless of whether we are in public, or in private around only those we know won't take offense, because language and colloquialisms are established through repetitive use in conversations and social contact and sometimes the best thing we can do, the safest thing we can do, is to stop the spread.

And if you were wondering how I could possibly link this back to the pandemic, there you go.

Stay happy and stay you.

Variety is the spice of life, and unfortunately Tesco is out of stock

5th April 2020

We find ourselves currently on day thirteen of the UK lockdown, and, although nothing has changed in this time, there has been a drastic change to the situation we find ourselves in, and this is because our attitudes have changed as we've settled into this new temporary way of living, and a situation is only ever what it is perceived to be.

We have grown in our comfort of using Zoom calls, or just picking up the phone to talk to friends; we have acclimatised to exercise classes being online while instructors have worked tirelessly to become comfortable with teaching online; we have picked up books that we'd been meaning to read for months, if not years; we have learnt to work from home in a way that many had not thought possible; and we have settled into routines that keep the days ticking by.

We have adjusted.

Now, that is not to say that we are all going to be happy with the situation we're in, there will, of course, still be many people struggling with day-to-day life right now, but one thing I think worth mentioning is that, while I have already stressed the importance of routines, variety is the spice of life, and this is something that I think a lot of people are sorely missing.

It has been hypothesized that there are six core human needs: certainty; uncertainty/variety; significance; connection; growth; and contribution; and these are what I want to discuss today, with a particular focus on uncertainty and variety.

Personally, I feel as though I am getting both contribution and significance through writing this blog and my wellbeing position at work. It's doing these things that allow me to feel like I am doing something special and unique (a.k.a. significant) that will provide support for others (a.k.a. contribution), and I know many of you have found your own ways of contributing; be that volunteering for the NHS, supporting loved ones, stepping up around the house to make meals, or doing the shopping – an even more noble task than ever before.

Many of you will be achieving your growth in much the same way by using this lockdown period to work on something you've been meaning to set aside time for, but kept putting it off for whatever reason; whether that's reading, or exercising, or learning a new language, or through developing your own ability of introspection, taking the time to focus on yourself through any form of meditation, or anything else that requires work and practice.

Connection is the one that has probably seen the most attention over the past two weeks as we have all been calling loved ones to check in on them and let them know we care.

But certainty vs uncertainty is the area where we may be losing our balance. In most ways, these two will make up a whole as no one thing can be both certain and uncertain, and as we look forward, there is so much that is uncertain right now – many people are worried about their jobs, and, if we aren't, we still don't know when life will be taken off hold; and anything that is certain about the future is disappointing because the only reason anything is certain right now is because it has been cancelled or because we are looking only far enough forward to know for certain that we will still be in lockdown.

This is one of the reasons why routines are so important, because they allow us to regain a certain amount of certainty that can certainly improve our wellbeing; but the only way to balance this effectively with a positive dose of uncertainty is through variety.

I was on a call with two friends a couple of days ago and when I asked one of them how the lockdown was going for him, his response was that it was fine, but it was just getting a little bit "samey", and so many people are going to be feeling the same way. I know the sentiment very much resonated with me, although I suppose that's fairly obvious seeing as how you've now read seven hundred odd words that I've written on the topic.

Now, I'm not going to give you any specific pieces of advice on how to obtain variety, because we're all different and will therefore appreciate various bits of variety in a varied way, but the beauty of that is that the easiest way to gain some variety is through the people around us. If we all have our own unique and established routines, then simply by inviting someone to join us for a part of that routine, or by asking to join a part of someone else's we can find that variety.

I just want to add one final thing on this topic, because last night, a Saturday night no less, we had one of our Friday night poker nights (which would have been variety enough) using a few forty-minute Zoom calls and PokerStars' online Home Games platform, and it did wonders in shaking up the "same-iness" of the lockdown. So, I just wanted to add a specific and personal thank you to Ross for setting that up.

Stay happy and stay you.

I've literally just written this because Marcus won't stop berating me for not writing more

10th April 2020

I've avoided talking about too much science, things such as what causes depression; in part because, although I have read up on this, there is a huge amount to say and I don't have the first qualification required to have any authority on the matter, but also in part because this isn't a medical journal, it's just me trying to cling onto a form of creative outlet.

Okay, these posts aren't quite the same as what is normally considered to be creative, such as the books I've written, but the creativity of writing is not just in the story you tell, it's also in the art of the transformation of thoughts, because this is all art is: taking the firing of neurones in the brain and translating them into another form that others can understand, that others can relate to, that will cause others to experience an emotional reaction.

That is art. And art is often confused for creativity, but creativity is what comes before art, because creativity is simply having the thoughts; it's the unabridged, untranslated, untouched pure thoughts that zip across the pathways within your brain.

Then, once you have creativity, and you combine it with art, then comes skill, and skill is being able to make this transformation of thought with grace and with a finished product that has the desired effect of the art.

In this sense, speech is an art form, of course it is. If you take a thought, translate it into a sentence, and then vocalise the sentence then you have completed each of the three aspects discussed above, and, provided your interlocuter has understood your sentence, then you have executed your art with skill.

With these posts, yes, on a basic level, I hope that you understand the words themselves, but in terms of the "desired effect", I'm also hoping that people will think about matters they'd previously not considered, come to understandings previously not thought to exist, and, if I'm being entirely honest, think of me as a better writer than they previously did. There was always going to be something selfish within my love of writing.

The motivation behind my books is slightly different: I just want people to feel; I'm honestly not sure how much I mind what exactly it is they ultimately feel. There are elements of seeking to educate and inform within my books, but really, I'm simply telling a story, and storytelling is something incredibly dear to me; but then, it's similarly precious to us all, because we all love a good story, and I believe there are a few reasons for this.

The first is that the "hero's journey" narrative arc — where the stage is set, a hero is introduced, they face a problem, they struggle, then they overcome this problem — is believed to be deeply embedded within our collective psyche and may have helped early humans to build trust and teach morality.

The second is that when we listen to character driven stories, it has been shown that our brains release oxytocin, a hormone prevalent in the forming of social bonds.

And the third comes from a study that found that people who read fiction are better able to understand and empathize with other people, and to see the world from their perspectives, meaning that we can actually teach ourselves to be better people simply by reading or listening to good stories.

A different study estimated that roughly 65% of all our communication comes in the form of storytelling; whether that's telling someone what happened that day at work, or explaining how you're feeling to someone as a result of an event, or even recounting that strange dream you had the other night. It's all storytelling.

And this pandemic has decimated our storytelling; how can we be the centre-staged orator we thrive off being when there are no new stories to tell, when nothing new is happening?

A few of you this week have asked me when the next post would be out – obviously, now, here it is. But the reason it took a while to write it was because I didn't feel I had anything new to say, so why say anything at all?

Two reasons.

The first is that apparently, discussing not having anything to say can lend itself to a reasonably long post – who'd have thought it… And second because

I remembered something I've said on an embarrassingly large number of occasions given that I seemed to have forgotten it this week: the greatest skill in storytelling is being able to imbue the mundane with intrigue.

This morning, I mindlessly wandered down the stairs, wondering how on earth I would fill the next four days, how on earth I could continue to find variety, how on earth I could reignite the love for life that I had felt slipping over the course of the week as work worked to grind me down.

I placed a mug under the spouts of the coffee machine, listening to the beans rattle in the tray as the machine whirred to life, wondering for a brief bleary-eyed moment if this machine was empathising with how I felt as the few unoriginal thoughts I felt I had rattled around my tray of an almost empty brain.

Given the countless nights I have found myself still unable to sleep after hours of thoughts scratching at my eyes, gripping to my muscles, and the hours I have spent practising meditation, I'd never have thought that I'd find myself frustrated by having an empty head, and yet that frustration was the only feeling I could identify as the spouts on the coffee machine sputtered out the final drops of my morning coffee.

Why did I tell you that? Well, because that was the story of me making my coffee this morning, ostensibly about as dull a story as is imaginable, but, I hope, you will have found it to have been at least somewhat intriguing, certainly more intriguing at least than "This morning, I had a coffee." – otherwise I should probably reconsider this whole writing malarkey – and by telling that story I was hoping to point out that there is so much more happening in each moment we live than we often give those moments credit for, and all we need to do to appreciate these simple moments for the glorious Iliadic epics that they really are is remember to be a little more present.

I could justify this simple instruction to be a little more present using the studies into the myriad benefits of meditation and mindfulness, but, I think there's a good chance I will do a full post on these at a later date, and the reason that fits in better with what I've been saying here is that I just want to hear more stories, because I've realised this is something I've been desperately missing lately.

I'll leave you with one final thought. I mentioned earlier that reading or listening to fiction can develop our empathy and understanding. This point highlights the value of the words my grandfather lived by for much of his life, and I hope they will help you with your storytelling while "nothing new" is happening: "Never let the truth get in the way of a good story."

The End.

Stay happy and stay you.

A little dose of positivity

19th April 2020

So, here we are, a couple of days into the three-week extension of the lockdown and the one question that keeps repeating itself in my head is "Am I doing enough?"; am I doing enough to ensure that I'm looking after my own mental health; am I writing enough; am I working hard enough, or am I letting myself get dragged down a little too much by the lack of motivation; am I doing enough to look out for others.

I think this is a good thing.

If I think back to previous depressions, there are thoughts on loop, but they are distinctly different, and they're not questions. They are the pistes through the trees that tell me "I am not enough", that "I am not cared for", that there is no prospect of improvement.

There have been significant advances in research around depression in recent times, and one area that has seen particular focus is the Default Mode Network (DMN), made up of the major hubs being located in the posterior cingulate cortex and precuneus, the medial prefrontal cortex, and the angular gyrus, and – to horribly oversimplify the medical research – this is thought to be the time traveller of the brain. It's the system that is active when remembering the past or considering the future, and it has been found to be more active in the brains of people with depression, which makes sense, because when you're in a depression, you spend almost all the time stuck on loops that leave you utterly disconnected with the present and with reality.

By asking the question "Am I doing enough?", I'm checking in with how I am feeling right now, I'm assessing how I am living right now, and I'm trying to be more reflective and aware.

And I can also see that the answer to this question is probably a simple yes.

Perhaps the only question which is only a tenuous "yes" is am I writing enough, because obviously it has been a week between this post and the last, but of course, if I'm not writing Paradise Lost every evening then at least it suggests that I probably am working hard enough. That, or I'm playing too much PlayStation… but I prefer the former option there.

There is also the issue that I've found myself running out of important and insightful things to say much quicker than I thought I would. Although, this isn't necessarily a bad thing because, since the writing of Perhaps If a couple of years ago, I have used writing as a way to process events and emotions until I come through the other side with a clearer mind and a deeper understanding, and so if I don't feel a burning desire to write, a large part of that will be because there is little or nothing that I feel I need to process and I am already feeling like I have a clear mind and a sense of calm.

Am I awfully bored of the lockdown? Yes. Am I missing cricket, football, and tennis? Desperately. Do I wish I could just have my life back? Of course, don't we all? But did this extension come as a surprise? Nope, not in the slightest. So, I do feel like I've already processed the situation and come to a point of acceptance.

And this probably answers both the question "Am I doing enough to look after my own mental health?" and the question "Am I writing enough?" because if I am feeling good, then, yes, I am doing enough. What a simple and effective test. Of course, though, that doesn't mean I can now stop what I'm doing, stop my daily meditation, stop my writing; it just means that I'm on the up and I should keep it up.

If any advice is going to come out of this somewhat rambling post, then it will be exactly that. Looking after yourself isn't something that you can do simply when you feel like crap about either yourself or your situation, it isn't about being reactive, it's about the constant upkeep and doing all these things I've talked about in the last eleven posts all the time, and it's remembering to remind yourself that you matter and that you are cared for, always.

And this leads me quite neatly into the final question I asked at the beginning of this post: "Am I doing enough to look out for others?"

To answer this, I thought I would share three stories with you. The first of which happened on Friday morning when a message came through on a group chat, asking how everyone was doing. The first response simply read "Surviving." and I wondered if this was the new version of the typically British response of "Fine." when asked how you are, which worried me a little, because of its possible negativity, so I decided to reply with a few more words.

My message read as follows:

This morning, as I pulled back the curtains and let the light flood in and illuminate the never-so-tidy corners of my room, I felt imbued with a renewed zest for life and a sense of overwhelming optimism. Today will be a good day. Not because it's Friday and the week is nearly over, simply because today is today, the only day that you can do anything. There's no longer any value in planning for tomorrow, yesterday has gone, and this just means the relative importance of today is so much greater.

Did the question require such an absurd reply, both in length and content? Obviously not. But it did make a couple of people smile, and this is the point I want to make. If you make someone smile, be confident in the knowledge that you are doing enough – it's as simple as that.

The second story goes back to the earlier post The Careless Colloquialisms, which, on the advice of my cousin Al, I sent to the colleague of mine who featured so heavily. I will admit that my hands were shaking a little as I sent it; I didn't want unnecessary confrontation, and I also didn't want me sending this over to come across as an attack, or to make him feel bad about himself. But it didn't. He read it and called me up to both thank me for sending it and to offer up a very sincere apology, which was an excellent mood booster.

The final story comes from my sister when I walked in on her FaceTime catch-up with my mum yesterday and she told me that, having read my blog, she found herself finding new variety to keep her life spiced up.

She told me that she'd decided to take the back roads on her route home rather than the main road.

Of course, that may seem a bit silly, but we laughed about it, and it reiterates the point that it is the small things that make a difference: a smile on a friend's face; a little dose of positivity; or a laugh between siblings.

You don't need to do much to make a big difference.

Stay happy and stay you.

I actually had fun this week

25th April 2020

There is only one thing that I want to talk about today, and that is Countdown. This week at "work" I organised and hosted an office tournament from our dining room table, and I think it may have been the most fun I've had at my company — in or out of lockdown. The contestants in the first round ranged from the newest joiners to the firm up to the most senior staff member in the office, but by the final we had whittled away until the two that remained were both very strong players; we were in for a treat, I knew that much. What I couldn't have predicted was quite how well it went.

I joined the video call where I would be hosting the final fully garbed in suit and tie – this was a serious event after all – a couple of minutes before the scheduled start time to find there were two or three people already eagerly awaiting the afternoon's event. Now, in my opinion, the most awkward part of any video call is the first few minutes while those who are on the call on time are waiting for the latecomers to tune in; what do you say; who do you talk to; should you just sit there on mute?

Don't worry. I had a plan for this – it was the Countdown Final after all. I clicked into present mode so those who joined would be able to see my screen, turned on The Final Countdown by Europe, and on my screen was a PowerPoint slide that read "This is the Gatwick Office Countdown Final. But it's also the Final Countdown. Play will start when the music ends and we're all super psyched up."

The most unnerving problem with present mode though is that you can't monitor the state of the call; I knew we were expecting about forty people to tune in to watch, but I couldn't see people tuning in, or, heaven forbid, tuning out. What if when the music stopped and I flicked over to the call I saw that there was no one there, and that our finalists hadn't even showed up?

The other unnerving element of present mode is that you can see no one – because you're showing everyone your screen, but everyone can see you if your camera is on, as mine was. And halfway through the five-minute anthem, my phone buzzes next to me with a message on our company's internal instant messaging platform: "This is hilarious". Well, that put my mind at rest, even though I knew I was grinning like a fool and everyone could see me.

Just in case the music wasn't getting people sufficiently in the mood, as The Final Countdown entered its final minute, I edited the slide that everyone was looking at, adding a final line to the bottom: "1 minute to go...." it read.

Was I still trying to psych the unknown number of viewers up at this point or just failing to contain my own buzzy excitement? Hmm, I'd like to think it was probably a combination of the two, but if I'm being honest, by this point, I was nigh on giddy with anticipation.

The final seconds of The Final Countdown that were counting down to the Countdown Final faded out and I flicked over to our video call to see more than fifty people had tuned in. Fifty! This now mattered; not because I now needed to be serious, but because there was now a duty to entertain. Well, it was time for my opening introduction.

"Welcome one and all to the Countdown Final. You will most likely know that the New Zealand Rugby team is nicknamed the all blacks, you may well know that the New Zealand cricket team is nicknamed the black caps, but did you know that the New Zealand badminton team, up until complaints were made and they had to make a change, was nicknamed the "Black Cocks". The Black Cocks. Well, there you go.

"Now, of course, the all blacks are almost always the favourites; the black caps have cultivated their underdog factor, but do we have a favourite or an underdog today? Let's find out as we meet the players."

I ran through some of our finalists' statistics from the tournament, invited them to talk about their mascots, and then welcomed our guest partner who was sitting in dictionary corner.

The first six rounds of the actual game then flashed by in what felt like seconds and, with the players neck and neck, it was time to go to an "ad break" – a chance for people (myself included) to grab themselves another beer, and, of course, I had a "top-up teaser" ready to go. "NUDEFRED – you'll get back what you deserve." (I've added the answer to the bottom of this post.)

Three minutes later and we were back in, I had a fresh Peroni in hand, and my suit jacket had come off, because, my god was it hot in the spotlight. Three rounds later, with our finalists continuing to push one another, it was time to go to Dictionary Corner and hear what our guest partner had to say.

His opening words utterly overwhelmed the giddy anticipation I'd felt half an hour earlier as he spoke on behalf of all on the call to thank me for my energy and entertainment value in running this tournament and made me know quite how much my efforts had been appreciated. Oh, how that moved me.

He then levelled that out by asking me quiz questions as retribution for the previous inordinately complicated quizzing I'd subjected my peers and colleagues to. Did I get any of his questions right? Nope. Not a one. But, and I was surprised to realise this, I not only didn't mind, but loved every moment of it; it was all entertainment for our audience after all.

Once dictionary corner's segment, and my embarrassment, was concluded, the game resumed and the final six rounds flowed smoothly, the jokes landing, the entertainment continuing, and before too long, we established a winner and it was time for my closing comments.

"Well, there we have it. Our undisputed, undefeated contestant becomes our undisputed, undefeated champion. Congratulations to you.

"However, that unfortunately means that that is it from us here. Thank you to all who took part, thank you to all who have watched from home, and from all of us here at the Countdown Studio which is my dining table, have a lovely weekend. Goodbye."

The thirty-second Countdown theme music played out one final time as I watched the viewers sign off the call, and as they did, my phone started buzzing again with messages thanking me for what had been an immensely entertaining event. I felt so grateful to everyone who had been a part and had helped make it such a success; we'd put on something so simple and yet so special.

And this is why I'm sharing this with you. Well, this and because I'm just trying to ride yesterday afternoon's high a little longer – not that there's anything wrong with that, I said that it was important to take the small wins where you could right at the beginning of this blog, and the only logical extension to that is to revel in the bigger ones for longer.

But, back to this "this" that I've mentioned; I stand by my earlier comment that this Countdown malarkey might have been the most fun I've had in my job, in or out of lockdown, and I wanted to use this story to point out that, however claustrophobic, however mood dampening, however boring and repetitive this lockdown gets, it is possible to have fun, it is possible to laugh, it is possible to live, and not just survive. All you need to do is take something you love, convince a bunch of people that they'll love it too, and then make them love it – doesn't get much simpler than that really, does it.

Okay, I'll admit, perhaps not as easy as it sounds, but if you take those little doses of positivity from last week, cultivate them, and share them, you might find yourself surprised at how many people will want to join you on your journey, whatever you're doing. I mean, who'd have thought Countdown would have been so popular! (Even if I do work in a company full of accountants… some of us are a lot more fun than the stereotype suggests, I promise!)

Well, there we have it. That's all from me, so, from all of us here at my blog to all of you reading at home, have a lovely weekend, and I'll see you next week.

Stay happy and stay you.

Refunded. Of course it was.

Guilt and mistakes

9th May 2020

It's been a couple of weeks since I last updated you with the things that have been going here, and, by "here", I of course mean in my mind, because what else really matters in the context of this blog other than what is going on in my mind.

So, as a quick update, I struggled this week. A part of that has to be put down to the fact that I didn't write anything last weekend, which means that I didn't do what I've found to be without doubt the most effective self-maintenance that I have at my disposal. I've already told you what writing, art, and stories all mean to me.

Another part, though, will be because I found myself struggling to get much quality sleep. And part of that has been because of some vivid and disturbing dreams, the most shocking of which hit me on Friday night when I dreamt that I was on a Zoom call with someone significant from my past.

Now, when I say "someone significant", what I mean is that I was on a call with the embodiment of all of the greatest mistakes that I've made in my life, the symbol of my deepest regrets, the most prominent reminder of the times when I've been in more pain than I can even reasonably comprehend today. And, he was also the spark for the one panic attack I've had.

I know, with certainty, that I was, at one point, as low as someone can get – I remember the event, and I know what the emotions that overwhelmed me in that time were; but there is a distinct emotional disconnect with that time, that night. I can't go back and feel how I felt in that time.

But this Zoom call, and how I felt when I woke up in the middle of the night, that brought me close.

When I answered the call, I wasn't even sure if he would be there on the other side, I didn't know if I wanted him to be there, but, if he was there, I didn't know if he would berate me, if he would point out all the reasons why he is justified in hating me, if he would remind me of all the reasons why I should hate myself.

But I answered the call, he was there, sat in a dark red chequered plaid shirt, smiling at me, and his opening words, oh how they've stuck with me, were "Hey mate, been a long time."

No wonder it's been a long time. His last message, one that didn't happen in a dream, but that I got in a Waitrose car park in Exeter, suggested that even eternity wouldn't be a long enough time.

But, on Friday night, back in Dream World it appeared that enough time had passed, and what little else I can remember of this call, that dimple-inducing smile, his soft tone, the sparkle in his eyes, it all showed me that he had forgiven me, and not in the platitudinal sense of the phrase whereby you know it will make someone feel better to think they've been forgiven, so you decide to be the bigger person and tell them that this is exactly what you've done, despite still holding onto little strands of resentment and bitterness.

He'd forgiven me in the sense that all was well.

And it broke my heart.

Why?

Well, if you're honest with yourself and you let yourself remember a time you've done wrong by someone, remember a time when you've been the cause of someone else's pain, a time when you've held onto that regret, and yet when confronted with the subject of that pain, they've forgiven you, I would expect that you would know the answer.

I hadn't forgiven myself. And, still, to this day, it appears that perhaps I hold those mistakes with me.

You may be hoping that I will tell you who this Zoom call was with, maybe you want to know what my deepest regrets are, or what I consider my greatest mistakes. I'm not going to share these; they're mine, and mine alone. Perhaps you're simply concerned that Zoom calls have permeated my subconscious to the point that they are now the way I dream about social interaction – believe me, it concerns me too.

What I will share with you though, what I think I have shared with you, is that I have made profound mistakes, I have hurt others – however unintentional causing that pain was, however unfortunately coinciding with my deepest struggles those mistakes were, however little I knew better – and I carry that burden with me.

I share this with you because there are three valuable lessons that come out of it – and none of them are that I am spending too much time on Zoom.

The first is that depressions breed guilt and mistakes. I've told you that someone in a depression is an entirely different person to the one you have come to know; I have told you how infinitely difficult it is to think straight within a depression; what I haven't explained to you is how when you come out of that depression, everything you did within it still feels like you, still clings to you as being your mistakes, being your failures. It is one of the ways that depression keeps you under water for so long: every time it pulls you down, you make another mistake, and, should you so much as try to take a breath, that breath will fill your lungs with reminders of all the ways in which you can justify thinking quite so little of yourself.

And the truth is that the responsibility, as always, still lies with you for your actions. That is just a part of being human. We will make mistakes, we will hurt others, and we will be responsible for these things we do.

What is vitally important to remember, however, is that the blame does not also lie with you. Actions may often speak louder than words, but remember that it is clothes that maketh the man, and we can change our clothes. And, by this, what I mean is that one action does not define someone. They may simply have been having a bad wardrobe day.

And this leads me into my second lesson; let's not be too quick to judge. A few weeks ago, I talked about ensuring that we strive to contextualise people's words; well, do the same with their actions. Remember that your loved ones are your loved ones for a reason, and that, among other reasons, is because they would never intentionally wish to cause you any pain. Remember this in the event of someone making a mistake.

Finally, try to do what I thought I had done and have spent the last day reconsidering, and will continue to try to do going forward: forgive yourself.

Take responsibility for your actions, yes, apologise sincerely, of course, but remind yourself, if you need to, that you are only human, remember that we all make mistakes, and know that you did not intend to cause hurt. Because, if you don't, you will only cause more hurt; you will only hurt yourself.

Look after those you love, remind yourself that you deserve to fall in that group, and, therefore, look after yourself.

Stay happy and stay you.

The End

19th May 2020

It's reached the point where it's time to say goodbye.

It's something that happens with practically everything you have or do in life and it's something that we've had to do a lot of in recent times. Be that to say farewell to something as simple as a weekly pub trip, or a team training session, or be that to say a final goodbye to a loved one.

Why am I ending this page? Why am I adding one more goodbye to the collection of painful and frustrating goodbyes we have already had to say?

Because it's time.

I've spoken my mind, I've shared my experiences with you, I've hoped to help you understand me better, and, in the process, understand yourselves better, and it's been a pleasure and a relief. This page has helped me through some difficult days, has helped me process some difficult thoughts, and has given me a space to feel a semblance of freedom in a world where such a feeling is a luxury. And I hope, with all I have, that through reading these posts, you have been able to find a breath of that freedom as well.

But, as you may have noticed over recent weeks, the wisdom and insights I have to offer have thinned out, and now, with it being mental health awareness week, there are only three things left that I feel I want to share.

The first, as an earlier post alluded to, is about what meditation is; the art of being present. The first thing I will say about meditation is that it is a skill as any other: it takes practice and refining; do not lose hope if you feel that you are struggling to achieve anything significant quickly. The second thing I will say is to reiterate that it is a skill as any other: you will be more receptive to certain coaching over other forms; if you find yourself achieving nothing, try a new coach or app or technique. The third thing I will say is to aggressively hammer home that it is a skill as any other: do not compare yourself to others; do not berate yourself for not achieving; do not give up.

It's possible that you glossed over that previous paragraph thinking that meditation isn't for you and are now hoping that this paragraph will move onto the second thing that I wanted to share. Well, we're not there yet. How could we be? That previous paragraph assumed that you knew what meditation was and were already practising; so, let's just take a moment to think about what meditation is.

I've already said that it is the art of being present, but, that is exactly the sort of wishy-washy nonsense that has creative-types mm-ing and nodding, and leaves the rest of the population a touch frustrated.

Let's start with this idea that meditation is an art. I've already described art as "taking the firing of neurones in the brain and translating them into another form that others can understand". What better way to think about meditation than being a way to translate your own thoughts into a form you can understand yourself. I've also talked about the importance of checking in with yourself; what better way to do that than to take the time to understand yourself and your thoughts.

What about this idea of "being present" then? Of course, we all exist in the present; the question I pose to you, though, is do you live there too? Are you aware of the breaths you take; are you mindful of the mouthfuls of your meals that you take; are you really present in the present?

Being present isn't just about noticing and taking note of your surroundings; it is equally – if not more so – about taking note of you: how you feel; what you're thinking; who you are. It's about knowing yourself, without getting lost in ideals of who you've been before and who you wish you could be in the future.

And this brings me neatly – almost as if I planned this – onto the second thing I wanted to discuss: how valuable meditation can be with regards to depression.

I have explained, most recently, that depression keeps you stuck on loops that breed guilt, that make you hate yourself, make you question your value, if you're lucky enough to be in a position where it's still a question.

Being mindful of your thoughts, while maintaining an awareness of those around you, while simultaneously taking the time to know yourself, and to know how wonderful you really are, makes it very difficult indeed to think little of yourself, while also making it difficult to be unaware of how much care and affection others have for you.

I have explained, in The Great White Mountain, how important it is to maintain the pistes of our minds, and I don't think that I need to go into much detail explaining how meditation is exactly the way in which I maintain the pistes of my mind.

I have also explained how depression creates both a break from reality and an utter disconnect from the present. I didn't, however, go into any detail about the ways in which your brain torments you by constantly bringing up those mistakes you've made, or by convincing you that whatever future you may want, there is no alternative to the life you're living now, leaving you living a life that is both painfully regretful of the past, because you can remember no past except for that which you wish you could forget, and that which has been distorted to present yourself in the worst possible light, or painfully frightened of the future, because there is no prospect of change. This is not a life that I would wish upon anyone.

Reconnecting with the present, breaking that fear of the future, and illuminating the past in the light which it was meant to be in, in which it was actually shot, all of it helps the brain avoid slipping into those depressive tendencies, into those self-perpetuating cycles of self-deprivation and self-harm, whether physical or otherwise.

Which, shockingly, leads me tidily onto the final thing I wanted to share before I wrap up this page.

I said in my previous post that I was, at one point, as low as someone can get.

There was a time when I didn't believe anyone wanted me on this planet, let alone wanted me around or wanted to help me. And there was a brief time when I thought that this thought was the truth within which I lived. And this was the time when I hoped my body wouldn't be able to cope with the release that I hoped it would take.

This week is mental health awareness week, and, in that spirit, I will now be very clear, I will make sure any of you reading this are abundantly aware. I tried to kill myself.

Depression is not about feeling a bit unlike yourself. Depression is not about feeling a bit bummed out. Depression is not about hoping for a bit of luck to finally swing your way.

It is being unable to recognise yourself. It is hating that person you don't recognise. It is the complete absence of hope.

But life, life is hope, and hope is life.

We are not, by any means, in a world cured of depression. But we are in a world that is starting to understand, and that gives me hope; gives me hope that one day we will be free of this.

And, with that, I will share my final message: be aware; make others aware; and be there. Be there in the present, be there for yourself, and be there for those you care about.

Stay happy and stay you.

End of Part One

Part Two

Notes to Work

Intrinsic and extrinsic motivations

17th September 2020

It's been a while now since I offered up any insights, advice, or guidance around mental health. In part, that is because I wore myself down and I needed to recover; in part, it's because the anticipated potential levels of depression and anxiety that could have come as a result of this virus crisis never came to fruition here at work, and we found ourselves able to find a new rhythm and routine that suited us just fine. And, because of that, you may be wondering what my plan is here, what I might want to achieve.

Well, during my own recovery time, one thing I wanted to achieve was to better understand the causes of depression and anxiety.

If you are reading this, then it is almost certain that you read the piece I put out for World Mental Health Day, the piece in which I described my emotional experience with depression, how it felt to be in that situation. I didn't describe how I got there, although I did allude to it, and, over the next eight weeks, I still won't share that with you; I will, however, be sharing with you the most common causes of depression and anxiety.

The one I want to start with is the balance between intrinsic and extrinsic motivation. The idea behind intrinsic and extrinsic motivations is a simple one: when you do something for the sheer joy you derive, that is intrinsically motivated; when you do something in order to gain something – money, property, sex – that is extrinsically motivated.

Of course, your day to day life within a job can blur the lines a little as you may enjoy doing what you are being paid to do; so, the way to work out how intrinsically or extrinsically motivated you are in your work is to imagine the scenario where you receive a living wage for yourself and any dependents you may have each year, regardless of the work you do, and then to ask yourself if you would still do the work you do.

Philosophers have been suggesting for centuries, if not millennia, that those who overvalue money and possessions, or who value their lives through the value placed upon them by the opinions of others, will be unhappy; but it wasn't until Tim Kasser approached this idea that any scientific backing was lent to this most obvious of concepts. And, yet, the results of Kasser's studies still managed to surprise those who saw them.

The first studies showed nothing particularly surprising: there was a much higher rate of depression and anxiety among those who valued money and possessions higher; and the emotional state on a day-to-day basis was significantly lower for those who were more materialistic, while the prevalence for illness or physical ailment was much higher.

The surprise came with Kasser's fifth study: he took 200 people across a broad demographic, and asked them to set out their goals; he assessed how materialistic and extrinsically motivated those goals were, and then asked the individuals to maintain a mood diary over the period of the study. Those within the study whose goals were more intrinsic – such as being a better friend, or make my kids laugh at least once every day – became significantly happier as they achieved their goals. However, those whose goals were more extrinsic – such as gain that promotion, buy that car, get that house – were noted to achieve no increase in their day-to-day happiness after achieving their goals. None.

Since Kasser there have been studies across the UK, Denmark, Germany, India, Romania, Australia, Canada, Russia, and South Korea that have all shown the same thing. There have been 22 studies showing a direct and significant link between materialism and depression, and a further 12 studies showing a similar link between materialism and anxiety.

It has been shown that the more extrinsically motivated we are, the shorter-lived our relationships are; it has been shown that the brain focuses inwards more, as you increase the amount you monitor and question yourself, while also only being able to derive comfort from external comparisons. And yet, there will always be someone with a faster car, with a bigger house, who's more talented, or who has a more attractive face, or body; and in spending so much time focussing on the things that will lead to misery, we compound the problem by not leaving enough time to focus on what does matter; on the things we do that are entirely intrinsically motivated.

But there is hope. Of course there is; this would be a god-awful series if it were just eight weeks of me moaning about how the world is burning around us. And the hope comes from the fact that our levels of materialism can fluctuate dramatically, and rapidly.

Take for example a study done in 1978 where a number of 4 and 5 year-old Canadian children were split in half, with half being shown 2 adverts for a particular toy, and the other half being shown no adverts at all. The children were then offered a choice: they were told they could either play with a really nice boy who had no toys; or they could play with a really nasty boy who had the toy featured in the advert. Unfortunately, those who had watched the adverts showed a strong preference for the nasty boy with the toy. Now, that was 2 adverts, and it was 1978. It is estimated that the average American is subject to 5,000 advertising impressions every day; be that anything from a TV advert to a Nike swoosh on a friend's shoes.

Okay, that is an example that goes in the wrong direction, highlighting how sensitive we are to suggestion, and how quick we are to abandon intrinsic values, but it also highlights how quickly we can fluctuate; and that means that with a bit of work we can push ourselves back to living by the values that actually make us happy.

So, how do we do that…? Well, one thing we can clearly do is to limit our exposure to advertising, and, when exposed, to be conscious of the subconscious effect it's having. But there is more we can do, there are bigger life changes we can make that can have big impacts on our happiness levels.

Now, I am obviously not suggesting that everyone who finds their job here a tad drab on the odd occasion to drop pens and split; that would be insane. What I am suggesting, though, is that we don't allow ourselves to be drowned by the extrinsic "goal setting".

Remember the study that followed the people who had set out their goals at the start; a large contributing factor to those people achieving their intrinsic goals was simply because they'd set them out, and they'd made a loose commitment to them.

So, this is what I suggest to you: take some time to think about what you are intrinsically motivated to do; make time for those things; and think of at least one thing you want to achieve that you will get nothing out of except for joy, because that joy, in its purity, is worth so much more than it is often given credit.

A hopeful future

24th September 2020

I explained in my World Mental Health Day piece that one of the ways in which depression can be so devastating is that it shatters your ability to see past how you currently feel, leaving you short-sighted and trapped in a painful present that you cannot believe will ever be different.

Interestingly, there has been significant debate around whether this myopia is more cause or effect: does someone become incapable of seeing a more positive possible future when struck down by depression or anxiety; or, does the belief that there is limited prospect for a brighter future lead to depression or anxiety?

The debate still continues, as it does with most questions around mental health, although I believe the answer is fairly simple, and, as the debate continues, I am going to pick a side. The loss of a sense of future is definitely a huge contributing factor to the dramatic rise in depression and anxiety over recent decades, and, then, those who slip into depressions will find their lack of ability to imagine themselves in the future cemented; someone will slide along the spectrum of future outlook from believing what comes next will be no better than now, up to the point that "what comes next" ceases to be something that exists.

Of course, holding this belief raises the question as to what has happened in recent times to foster this diminishing sense of security and a hopeful future. Well, you really don't need to look far to work it out, and it is inextricably linked to the rise of the precariat.

While in the UK, those on zero-hour contracts make up only 3% of the workforce, that figure may be as high as 20% in other Western countries such as Germany or USA; self-employment accounts for over 15% of the workforce in the UK; Covid-19 has obviously left many more unemployed; there has been a systematic erosion of union powers; and UK household debt is on the rise, with the average debt per capita now over £31,000, which is, of course, higher than the median household income of £29,600 in 2019, and is leading to an increased number of people across the classes living on a pay-check-to-pay-check basis.

There is little doubt in my mind that we, as a global economy, have been steadily removing people's sense of security little by little, consistently, and continuously.

In the 1970s, the liberal Canadian government embarked on an experiment, with the 17,000 inhabitants of a rural town called Dauphin their guinea-pigs.

The wealth of this small farming town at the time was almost entirely dependent on the success of a crop called canola; when the crop did well, the town did well; when the crop was poor, the people were poor.

The experiment was simple: every adult was given a basic living income, that would be roughly $20,000 in today's money, with no strings attached. It was enough to cover housing and food, but not to cover luxuries.

The interesting relevance of $20,000 comes in a study by Cohen and Timimi in 2008 that showed those who were earning an annual salary less than this figure were more than twice as likely to become depressed as somebody making $70,000 or more.

So, with the context laid down, let's consider the results of this experiment. The first thing to note was the fundamental culture and mentality shift that led to the women feeling empowered to study at a university level; students in general stayed in school longer, with performance data showing marked improvements; the number of low-birth-weight babies declined; parents stayed home longer after having babies; and overall work hours fell a small amount as people spent more time focusing on their intrinsically motivated activities. But, more than all of that, the prevalence of depression and anxiety (as measured by visits to the doctors citing mood disorders) fell dramatically.

Not only were people's level of security effectively insured, but this basic income meant that the more tedious jobs had to offer more perks and better conditions in order to maintain employment, and, as these jobs became more appealing, it meant that the key and yet mundane work, such as sanitation, was still done within this community. More than this though, people would feel empowered to retrain, to study further in order to follow the dreams and ambitions they had.

Now, is it closer to a pipe dream than a realistic suggestion to offer up basic incomes to every individual? Probably, yes, not least because it would deepen the people's reliance on the state – something that worries me greatly; (although Rutger Bregman might disagree, and I would highly recommend his book Utopia for Realists if you are interested in this topic), but, is it not also the case that every dream for a more civilised society starts in that way? If you'd told people in the 1950s that you believed in a world where members of the LGBTQ+ community would not just not be discriminated against, beaten, murdered, and forced to hide in themselves and in society, but that they would be considered as equals and would be able to be open and happy, you would have been laughed out of town. And yet, here we are.

Of course, this is a series written for you, so, how does all of this apply to us here in this office, other than simply being an interesting read, when the reasons for the rise of the precariat barely apply to our positions? I would say there are two factors to consider: the first is that many of us will have friends and family who are affected by zero-hour contracts, or feelings of a lack of security, especially at this time, and a better understanding of their situations will only increase our empathy levels; and the second is because we are not immune to the possibility of not being thrilled by the future laid out before us, or feeling insecure in those futures.

I know, for example, of one manager in a different office who held very little savings and would fail to be able to pay his rent within one month should he leave his current role; and many of us will also remember the sense of dread around the exams, and the anxiety we felt over failing those exams and being asked to leave.

Which leads me on to my closing guidance: should you feel inspired to find a practical way of initiating the "pipe dream" of global freedom and security, good luck, and please share with me your thoughts, because I am well aware that I'm condemning our current system without suggesting any alternative that might work; but, and this is much more likely to be relevant, keep an eye on that sense of hopeful future. If you find yourself losing touch with it, speak up – either to a friend, a therapist, or your people manager; if you find yourself feeling weighed down by the path you're currently on, rather than excited, speak up – again, to anyone you think might help; because, and this is worth remembering, there is always something you can do that will reignite that spark for life; sometimes, we just need to remind ourselves that it exists.

Status and respect

1ˢᵗ October 2020

The main focus of today's piece will be on the work of neuro-endocrinologist Robert Sapolsky on stress, and I would highly recommend that you look deeper into his work if you find what I say here interesting.

In particular, it's his research with baboons that I want to discuss. He spent years studying baboons in the Serengeti and made various important discoveries that started with how their hierarchical system works: each male has a rank within their troop, from number one being the alpha, right down to the bottom of the pile; while each female inherits their social status from their mother.

What this rigidly structured hierarchy means is that one baboon who is ranked four, for example, can take a nice shady spot that the baboon ranked five is sat in; five can then go and find six and take the female they're mating with; six can then go and find seven and take the juicy mango that they're enjoying for their lunch; and so on, and so on.

Once Sapolsky had determined the intricate machinations of the hierarchical system, he decided to investigate what this structure meant for the cortisol levels (the prominent stress hormone) in the troop by taking blood samples over an extended period of time. What he found was that there was (almost) always a perfect inverse correlation between rank and stress: the lower your status, the greater your stress.

The exception to this correlation came when there was a power struggle in progress. In this case, as the higher ranked baboons felt their status threatened, their cortisol levels soared. This will become relevant later when we start to draw comparisons to modern human living.

But let's keep our focus on the bottom ranked baboons for now, because Sapolsky also noted a significant difference in their behaviour from the rest of the troop: he noticed that they exhibited something called subordinance gestures. They would move slower, keep their heads lower, and occasionally go so far as to crawl on their bellies.

It was psychologist Paul Gilbert that took this idea a little further, spotting the similarities between this behaviour and the way a human being suffering from depression acts, and hypothesising that depression is in itself a submission response. Much like the bottom ranked baboons would exhibit subordinance gestures to signal to the rest of their troop that they will offer no challenge and that they are of no threat, human beings suffering from depression are showing the same signals.

The question is then posed as to what humans are submitting to, as to what has created this submission response; and, in my opinion, and upon reflecting on Sapolsky's work with the baboons, it is beyond doubt that the hierarchical system we have developed in society in the majority of the Western world is a massive factor.

Today, there are eight billionaires with the same combined wealth as the bottom half of the global population; although, of course, it is important to note that it is wealth we're talking about here, not cash, and that wealth in itself often translates into jobs for many more people, but the statistic does highlight the extent of inequality that exists in the modern global economy.

But it isn't just inequality of wealth that is important here, it is also the inequality of perceived status and respect. The way corporate structures work across the majority of the modern world leads to a select few "top ranked" people for a very many "bottom ranked" individuals.

The interesting aspect of inequality in the human economy though is that it impacts everyone in a negative way. To gain a much better understanding of this idea, I would suggest that you read The Spirit Level by Richard Wilkinson and Kate Pickett, but, to dramatically oversimplify one of the important findings from their research, it is not just the many "bottom ranked" people whose stress levels are affected by inequality, but also everyone above them. As we have been drip-fed the importance of status through our every-day living, be that via social media, any other form of media, or simply the way we believe that others will value us based on our positions and success, we have also had a new way of thinking embedded within us: our status is constantly under threat.

The research Wilkinson and Pickett conducted involved sifting through enormous amounts of data, and the most significant discovery they made was that there wasn't just a correlation between inequality and stress, but there existed a correlation between inequality and all forms of mental illness.

Today, in our own society, we have a rigid hierarchical status structure that is comparable to that of the baboons, only without the violent fights that establish our rankings. And the disappointing fact is that, as human beings with choice and intelligence, we have no real need for the levels of inequality that we see in today's world. Why would we choose a system that creates so much mental suffering? The argument is, often, because it generates the most wealth; but how can that be possible when it is people that generate wealth and, right now, we are seeing so many people suffer?

But this is all very general, so let's focus in and see how this relates to us here at work. Of course, we have an established hierarchy here as well, from partner down to associate, or intern; but, in my experience, this hierarchy is not a social one, as the P&Ds are respectful, welcoming, and approachable; no, the hierarchy we see here is much more of a very reasonable knowledge-based one where everyone knows they are appreciated and have a role to play in the work we do.

I think, although there is an element of income inequality, the true relevance to us here at work comes in perceived perceptions of ourselves: do we all know that we are valued for who we are and not for our position in the firm?

This is my parting message today: be confident in the fact that this is the case; you are not valued based on your grade, or on your extrinsic achievements, you are valued because of you, whatever your grade. Be conscious of the fact, and remind yourself, that you don't value your friends in that way, so why would your friends value you in that way; and, on the very infrequent situation where someone may treat you in such a way that you lose confidence in this message, whether at work or not, then you should feel confident in reminding yourself that in treating you that way, they are quite literally no better than a baboon.

Hidden pasts, shame, and grief

8th October 2020

The title of this instalment might suggest there are three things that I want to discuss today, but, really, it's just two – trauma and grief – and, even then, the two often come together and can be discussed as one topic: pain and suffering.

For too many people, and far too often, we create a distinction between what might be considered "natural" pain and suffering, and depression. We consider depression to be a mental illness while considering pain and suffering to be a natural cause and effect response; and yet making this distinction is fundamentally wrong, wildly unhelpful, and largely unfounded.

The first study I'm going to share with you today was carried out by Dr Vincent Felitti in California in the 1980s on significantly overweight individuals. The study started out as a dietary experiment that acted as an analysis of how quickly people could lose weight if they were given no food and were required to live off supplements (potassium, magnesium, protein, and vitamin C), water, and their own stored body fat.

On a physical level, the experiment worked wonders: for example, there was one woman who came into the study at 185kgs and who, after just 51 weeks, weighed a healthy-for-her-height 60kgs.

And yet, Felitti noticed something he thought very peculiar: many of those who'd shed their weight quickest during the study were sinking into panics, rages, and depressions, then quitting the study and quickly replacing the weight they'd lost. So, Felitti decided to try and work out why this was happening, and, knowing that changes in appetite was one of the major symptoms of depression, he began by asking his subjects why they were getting fat.

He found that the vast majority of the participants had experienced severely traumatic childhoods, with 55% having been the victims of sexual abuse when they were younger, and that many felt that their weight provided protection. It was a mechanism to keep sexual attention and focus off them. Felitti also noticed that there was a sentiment that maintaining a healthy body was not particularly important given a loss of a sense of a hopeful future as discussed a couple of weeks ago.

For me, it is not the dramatic findings Felitti made that is most shocking about this, it is that today we have in this country both a rising mental health crisis that is desperately underfunded and dangerously misunderstood, and a rising obesity crisis that we think will be fixed by taxing fast foods and investing in sport. Much like most of the work around mental health, it's a good start, but it's kind of missing the point.

The second study I want to share with you is the ACE (Adverse Childhood Experiences) study that was conducted by Dr Robert Anda and consisted of asking a sample of 17,000 individuals in San Diego if they'd experienced any of ten different categories of childhood trauma, from neglect through to sexual abuse. He found, unsurprisingly, that there was a correlation between the number of categories of trauma experienced and the likelihood of experiencing a depression later in life; however, the correlation was exponential, with those who had experienced six of the ten categories of trauma being five times more likely to become depressed than those who'd experienced none, and those who'd experienced seven of the ten being thirty-two times more likely to attempt suicide at some point in their life.

The reason this study is so important is because it evidences a dose-response effect that shows that depression is just as much a natural response to events as grief, or what might be considered "natural pain and suffering", is.

Some of you will have heard of the DSM (Diagnostic and Statistical Manual), the medical bible for mental health disorders, where the nine major symptoms of depression are listed out in a somewhat callous checklist, and where medical professionals are told that someone needs to have been experiencing at least five of these symptoms for a period of time to be diagnosed as depressed. However, there is a caveat in the depression entry in the DSM called The grief exception which was added because it was noted that those who experience traumatic loss, such as the death of a child, exhibit the same symptoms in their grief as those listed out for depression – quite understandably so. The horror comes in the fact that this exception is only applied for two weeks; meaning that if you were to grieve the loss of a child, something a parent would reasonably never truly recover from, for longer than two weeks, you would be clinically diagnosed as mentally ill, suffering with a condition from which you need to recover.

I am, quite clearly, on the side of the debate that believes this is utterly nonsensical; but it also seems odd at this point to consider that grief in this extreme sense is the only applicable exception. Why would a relationship with a loving partner of a number of years or decades coming to an end not also be applicable, for example? Why is it that, as a response to losing that relationship, showing the same symptoms is automatically a sign of mental illness?

Before we go on, I'd just like to take a moment now to reflect on the noticeable difference between the childhood trauma discussed in the first half of this piece and the grief discussed in the latter half: the delayed impact. The studies around childhood trauma investigated the likelihood to experience depression later in life; while when grief is considered, it is the immediate response that is examined.

One thing that Dr Anda noticed when he conducted the ACE study was that a huge majority of his respondents had never discussed their childhood traumas before; further, he discovered that the reason they'd never discussed their experiences before was because they'd felt a sense of shame for their traumas, both unfathomably and also sadly understandably placing some or all of the responsibility for their experiences on themselves.

It is this idea of shame that leads me to the final study I want to briefly share with you today; during the AIDS crisis, researchers found that openly gay men with AIDS would live, on average, two years longer than those suffering from the disease who were similarly progressed and receiving the same treatment but were closeted, and the reason I want to share this study is because it highlights how devastatingly powerful an emotion shame is. And in knowing this, it is also vitally important to know that there is a fine line between being receptive to the severity of someone's reaction to an event, their grief, and imposing upon them the notion that that grief is more mental illness than natural response, as opposed to being both in full and equal measure, and, in doing so, creating a sense of shame in having that natural response. It is this fine line that too many overstep when it comes to depression and anxiety.

And so, onto my closing comments. Let us remind ourselves that we will not know everything that someone has suffered through or experienced, and, because of this, remember to withhold judgement, replacing it instead with compassion and empathy. Second, know that anything that happened to you as a child is neither your fault, nor something you need to carry any shame for. And, finally, be aware that depression is often a very understandable and natural response and, as such, is never something you should feel ashamed of.

The natural world

15th October 2020

This week's instalment focuses on an idea that I'd be surprised if anyone among you is not already aware of: the human need for the natural world. And, as a relatively well researched topic, I have plenty of papers and studies to share with you this week.

To begin with, I'm going to tell you about evolutionary biologist Isabel Behncke's research into bonobos, during her time with Oxford University, at Twycross Zoo and in the Congolese rainforest.

While she was working at the zoo, she'd noticed various concerning behaviours in the more unhappy of the bonobos that she only realised was unnatural once immersed in their natural habitat in the rainforest. The low status and marginalised bonobos in the rainforest would develop ticks, scratch themselves, and spend less time grooming themselves; but when removed from their natural habitats and placed in captivity, the ticks became compulsions, and the scratching could persist until the bonobo would bleed. It was this comparison that led her to conclude that the bonobo depression equivalent was limited in the extent to which it could develop while in its natural home.

Similar trends have been noted across many species: elephants have been known to grind their tusks, a source of great pride for them, against cage walls to the point of leaving no more than a stump; dramatic decreases in libido are documented across many, many species kept in captivity; and parrots have been known to pluck their own feathers, the bright colours of which are often the focal point of mating rituals. So why would the response in humans be any different? Because we're not in cages? There would be a significant number of people who spent much of the last six months in small flats in London who might see the irony of that.

However, it is also especially those people who will understand and appreciate the value that simply going for a walk or getting some fresh air can have, while the rest of us will at least have a conceptual appreciation for this. What may not be quite so well known is the research that supports this. A paper by Marc Berman et al. looked at exactly this, what the effect of taking a walk in nature had on concentration levels and mood across two groups: those who had depression; and those who did not. The disparity across the groups was striking, with the improvement in concentration and mood in the group of those who had depression being five times greater.

Another study, this time coming out of the University of Essex, looked at 5,000 households who had either moved from a rural area into the city, or from the city to a rural area, and compared the levels of depression across the two groups, noting, quite predictably, a dramatic increase in the levels of depression of those moving into the city, and a dramatic decrease in the levels of depression of those moving to rural areas.

Now, of course, there could be other factors at play here; for example, there is an increased probability that those moving into the city are moving for work, and an increased probability that that work will be more stressful than those in rural areas. There is also likely to be a greater sense of community in rural areas when compared to urban hubs, as well as the opportunity to live in larger houses with more space when moving out of the city.

It is because of these uncontrolled variables that Catherine Ward Thompson et al. published their paper comparing the depression levels in various deprived inner city communities that were as similar as is possible but for the fact that some had green spaces, such as parks or commons, while others did not. Their findings, you won't be remotely surprised to hear, were that the levels of depression in the communities that had green spaces were significantly lower.

The final study I want to share with you this week was documented in Howard Frumkin's paper Beyond Toxicity: Human Health and the Natural Environment, in which he describes his findings from an experiment involving inmates in the State Prison of Southern Michigan; a prison where, simply by chance because of the architecture, half the inmates' cells faced a brick wall, and the other half faced rolling farmland and trees. In his study, it was found that the inmates whose cells faced the farmland were 24% less likely to become physically or mentally ill.

In today's world it is very easy to pay the ego too much attention and lose sight of where we stand in the bigger picture; we are told of the importance of introspection, of self-analysis, of self-awareness, and of setting goals and making plans. All of this is important, yes, but it comes at a price without a genuine appreciation of the context, because when all of our focus is inwards, and when the entire picture presented to us is of ourselves, then the problems and struggles we have and face will seem vast.

However, when we find ourselves in the natural world, connected with genuine vastness, be that standing on an African savannah or atop a hill in the Lake District, or even gaining a sense of that vastness walking through Battersea Park, it's much harder to feel caged or trapped, it's much harder to feel lost, and it's much harder for those struggles to inflate large enough to block the view.

Given the number of responses on the World Mental Health Day pledges form that came through on Friday citing getting outside for fresh air or exercise, I don't feel the need to offer any specific words of wisdom on this topic; instead, I will just let you enjoy the education and feel confident that in getting that fresh air and getting outside you really are looking after yourselves.

Loneliness

22nd October 2020

This is the slightly edited version that was published in Lockdown Sceptics on 5th January 2021

This topic is a particularly interesting one for a number of reasons: first, because you're probably thinking, "Of course loneliness is a major cause of mental illness, so why should I spend five minutes reading about something I already know?" – read on and find out; second, because we are all aware of quite how particularly pertinent it is right now; and, third, because it was the most significant factor in my experience with depression.

Before we go any further though, I think it would be a good idea to explain what loneliness is, because it isn't as simple as not having friends or being alone. It is a process within the brain that has been designed by evolution that gives you a feeling as a result of believing you have limited or no connections that provide a sense of mutual aid and protection with other individuals.

Human beings began as a species on the savannahs of Africa but survived as a species because of cooperation and tribal support. If you were an individual who became separated from your tribe, no one would care for you should you fall sick, you would be unable to hunt effectively, and you would be vulnerable to predators; and it is because of this that the brain developed a way to send an urgent signal to reconnect with your tribe in the form of loneliness and a sense of insecurity.

In today's world, however, the connection that we need is slightly different: mutuality remains a necessity, and aid and protection are still important, although these come as a by-product of simply caring for one another; but avoiding loneliness is also about sharing something that matters to both sides of the connection, which gives rise to an interesting facet of loneliness: it has varying degrees not just in intensity but also in breadth.

Take, for example, three things I care deeply about: writing; cricket; and the queer community. I have people I discuss literature with, and I have people with whom I swap articles and pieces of work with; I have friends I play cricket with, and I have friends waiting around the corner to go to cricket with; but I have no queer community. Somehow, I have ended up with no friends - who would really truly understand - with whom I can discuss the struggles our community faces internally and externally, or the wondrous strides that have been made, or anything else that can be "explained" but cannot be genuinely understood by someone outside of the community, someone who hasn't lived it, and, because of this, I often feel intensely lonely in this very important aspect of my life.

But that's enough about me for now, because it's time I shared some of the science – suspend scepticism, if you please – around the effects of loneliness. The first comes from a paper by John Cacioppo and William Patrick, Loneliness: Human Nature and the Need for Social Connection (2008), in which participants were asked to spit in a tube and note down how lonely or connected they felt in that moment nine times a day. This allowed their cortisol levels to be measured and plotted against their levels of loneliness. What the data suggested was that an acute sense of loneliness produced the same amount of stress as when someone experiences a physical attack by a stranger.

Six years later, Cacioppo published another paper on loneliness that documented the long-term health impact was just as dangerous as obesity; and Lisa Berkman in 2015 published The Village Effect: Why face-to-face contact matters, which showed the risk of cancer, heart disease, and respiratory problems were all increased in individuals experiencing loneliness, concluding that loneliness makes us two to three times more likely to die on any given day.

But none of this answers the question as to whether loneliness is a cause or an effect of depression, and so Caciappo performed a further study over a number of years where participants were given an extensive personality test a number of times over the years to gauge those who had suffered, or were suffering, from depression as well as their levels of loneliness.

What he discovered was a lag between feeling lonely and experiencing a depression that confirmed loneliness preceded depression. Moreover, he was able to create a scale of loneliness and plot the chances of an individual experiencing a depression against that scale finding that were someone to move along the loneliness scale from feeling "50% lonely" to "65% lonely", their chances of developing depressive symptoms increased eight times.

Following this study, the believed progression of loneliness became established: an individual loses meaningful connections and becomes lonely; this loneliness creates a sense of insecurity (that may develop into anxiety) that causes a retreat from society; the retreat from society reinforces the lack of connections and develops into depression; the depression creates a belief that no one will care enough about them for a connection to ever be established again.

It's a frighteningly familiar story, and a story that has been forced upon individuals in the last nine months.

One rebuttal I've heard very often when discussing mental health, and one that always frustrates me, is the suggestion that depression and anxiety may not have actually increased in recent times, people are just more comfortable talking about it today. It's particularly frustrating because it's very difficult to disprove directly. However, it is possible to disprove by proxy when it is accepted that loneliness is a major cause of depression and anxiety, as there are many, many studies showing that loneliness has increased dramatically over recent times.

One of these features in the M. McPherson et al. paper, "Social isolation in America: Changes in core discussion networks over two decades" (2004), that asked individuals how many close friends they had that they knew they could rely on. At the start of the two decades, the modal response was three; at the end of the study, the modal answer was none.

All the evidence suggests that loneliness has been on the rise as a result of our movement away from community and tribe-like living; group activity engagement and community participation have been on the decline for decades; and we started replacing genuine face-to-face connection with screen-mediated contact that simply does not meet our psychological needs as human beings long before the Covid-response crisis, allowing ourselves to be fooled that we have enough connection by the little short-term dopamine hit we get when our phones buzz and that little notification pops up.

There are ways in which we can make our world just a little less lonely though. The first focuses on your passions; once you know what they are, be vocal about them and share them with those around you – you will find someone to share that passion with you quicker than you might think; and, if it is something that can be done in a group like playing a sport, or music, then make that time available so you can do it – that community is *vitally* important, and I do not use that word lightly.

The second focuses on looking after those around you; remember that the centre of a meaningful connection is mutual aid and protection, a sense we get from caring about someone and knowing that they care about us too. It takes next to nothing to remind someone you care about that you do care about them, and it does wonders to keep that truly toxic feeling of loneliness away.

Meaningful work

6th November 2020

This week is the final piece in this series, so, before I continue, I want to say that I hope you've enjoyed it and that you've found it informative, and, if you have any questions or want to discuss any part of this series, please do feel free to message me or drop some time in my diary.

Initially, when I was planning this series, I decided to leave this topic until last out of a worry that I wouldn't find it particularly easy to strike the right tone discussing with work how the lack of meaningful work is a major cause of depression and anxiety, especially as I have, on more than one occasion, felt a little disengaged with my role here at work.

However, my occasional disengagement is largely due to the very subjective factor that I need to be writing, and, well, here we are at the end of an eight-week series of 1,000-word articles that I've written just for you. More than that though, as my research into this topic expanded, it became clearer just how well we are doing here at work when it comes to engagement.

And that leads me into the first study that I think is very much worth sharing; it was conducted by Gallup and is written up in the William Davies paper, The Happiness Industry: How the Government and Big

Business Sold Us Well-Being (2016), and is essentially a global Pulse survey. The survey gathered data regarding people's engagement with work from millions of workers across 142 countries and the results were staggering.

Gallup defined "engaged" workers as being enthusiastic about and committed to their work, as well as being those who contribute to their organisation in a positive manner. They defined "not engaged" workers as those who are sleepwalking through their workday, putting time – but not energy or passion – into their work. And they defined "actively disengaged" workers as being those who are busy acting out their unhappiness at work, effectively seeking to undermine the organisation where they work.

The results of this study revealed that only 13% of workers are "engaged", 63% are "not engaged", and 24% are "actively disengaged". Let's pause on that for a moment; very nearly a quarter of the global workforce is actively seeking to undermine the company they work for in their day-to-day work life, and only 13% of the working population feels genuinely positive about the work they do.

To put that into perspective, the recent Pulse survey told us that in Gatwick audit, the engagement levels are at 78%. That is a striking variance.

I won't speak for our remaining 22% (which, with the same ratios between not engaged and actively disengaged would be split 16% and 6% respectively), but the most extensive research into how the work we do affects us, and why that global 87% (not engaged and actively disengaged) is quite so high, was performed by Michael Marmot and his team during the Whitehall Studies.

In the civil service, everyone is doing a desk job and is paid well enough to live and not be poor, but everyone in the civil service is also divided into slots on a strict scale that determines how much they are paid and what their status is, and this rigid structure meant that Whitehall provided as ideal a setting as is possible for this sort of research.

The two major studies that Marmot and his team embarked on extended over many years and looked at 18,000 civil servants in depth, spending at least an hour one-on-one with each of those 18,000 workers.

The first study looked into stress levels and the risk of heart attack when compared to the worker's ranking within the scale and the major finding was that those at the top of the ladder were four times less likely to have a heart attack than those at the bottom; more than that though, the study revealed that this inverse correlation extended down the ladder in a close relationship meaning that every step down the ladder you went, the higher your risk of a heart attack.

The second study looked at control; what would be the impact if two people worked at the same pay level, with the same status, in the same office, but one had a lower degree of control over their work in terms of freedom to choose work or methodology. What this study revealed was that control was vitally important: the workers with less control were found to be a lot more likely to become depressed or develop severe emotional distress.

Across the studies it was also found that there was a large spill-over into the workers' personal lives: the higher ranked individuals had more friends and engaged in more social activities after work. This wasn't, however, because they could afford to do these things (be that because of time or money) while the lower ranked workers couldn't; it was because the lower ranked individuals simply wanted to slump at the end of the day, collapse in front of the TV and not go out to see anyone.

These studies led a revolution around what stress at work looks like and took the view of stress to the point where it was concluded that the kind of work that causes stress is not about when an individual has to bear a lot of responsibility, it is when a worker is having to endure monotonous, ennui-inducing, soul-destroying work each day; it is when the work they do touches no part of them that they identify as being who they are.

A few years ago, there was an issue with the prevalence of suicide within the government's tax office and so the government brought back the same individuals who conducted the Whitehall studies, and Marmot found himself once again in long conversations with civil servants, and, through conducting these conversations with the tax officers he discovered that there were certain aspects of the tax work these civil servants were performing that were having a major impact on their mental health. The in-trays never seemed to get any smaller: at the end of each day, more work would be waiting for them than when they started their days, and, because of this, none of these workers enjoyed taking holiday, as time off simply made the situation worse. But the biggest driver of their suffering was that no one ever thanked them for their work. Marmot discovered through these conversations that a lack of balance between efforts and rewards was a major contributor to depression.

But all of this further highlights how we are doing comparatively very well here in Gatwick: not only are our engagement levels six times higher than the global engagement levels; but I am yet to come across a manager who isn't interested in an idea a junior team member has if they want to do the work they've been given in a slightly different way; I have the freedom to do things like writing this series; and we have a devoted recognition team to ensure we work towards and maintain a balance between efforts and rewards.

That said, there will always be disengagement as a result of what I mentioned earlier when I said that the type of work that causes stress is when the work you do touches no part of you that you identify as being who you are.

Audit, accountancy, or tax is not for everyone, of course it isn't; but that doesn't mean we can't do what we can to improve our chances of feeling engaged, whether that's talking to someone about changing the work you're doing, or how you're doing it, sharing an idea you have about ways of making improvements, finding something you can do that you do feel engaged with, or talking to the recognition team about ways that you might better feel appropriately valued and appreciated.

Because this is essentially what it boils down to: the more in control you feel and the more valued you feel, the more engaged you will be.

And that, sadly, concludes our eight-week series.

Before I completely wrap up though, I feel it would be helpful to make a couple of final points. The first thing I want to say is that what I have said over the last eight weeks is a combination of data, interpretation, and speculation, and that means that you are fully entitled to disagree with anything I've said -- although, if you do, I would very much like to hear why. The second thing I believe is worth clarifying is that what I've said over the last eight weeks is by no means exhaustive; there will be other social causes of mental health issues; these were just the major and most common causes in today's world.

It is also important to say that the topics I've discussed are not definitive. Having a number of these social causes present in someone's life does not mean they will necessarily experience a depression or suffer from anxiety; nor will an individual with only one of these social causes present in their life necessarily not suffer. There is evidence to suggest that there is a dose-response effect with these causes, that the more that are present, the more likely an individual is to suffer from mental health issues, but as many of you will know, one cannot extrapolate sample evidence back to the individual level.

But these social causes are present in today's world, and, as such, it is vitally important that you know that if you are struggling at the moment, or if you find yourself struggling in the future, you should not feel guilty about that, you should not feel weak. You should know that you are not abnormal, and you are absolutely not alone.

Measures and Mental Health

12th November 2020

When I asked you last week what further topics you'd like me to look into, you gave me two very interesting topics that would work as standalone pieces; however, one of these would, unfortunately, require a psychiatrist. The other was whether the government's pandemic response was "worthwhile [specifically] with respect to mental health", and that is what we are going to look at in detail this week.

However, it will be necessary to first accept that it is far beyond my expertise to be able to conclude within this piece whether or not the measures imposed are "worthwhile"; instead, I will be collating relevant data and research and concluding in the way data reports should be concluded: "on the uncertainties in the data" and "where there may be errors in the estimates" (as described by Carl Heneghan, Director of the Centre for Evidence-Based Medicine); and not in the way that the conclusions in various government-commissioned papers have been advising on policies.

The first thing that requires consideration is what the narrative of information is, including what remit those advising government have, and the answer is that there is only one point of focus: COVID-19. SAGE, made up of now 98 individuals, looks solely at what the virus is doing, and what developments might occur. This is why we are not seeing the peer-reviewed and detailed cost-benefit analyses that Theresa May demanded in her impassioned speech during the Lockdown 2.0 commons debate last Wednesday: it simply isn't within anyone's job description to look at anything other than the impacts of the virus and the impacts of restrictions on the virus. This is also why we have seen no additional government funding to the NHS for mental health impacts since the £5m announced in May; an amount that, even combined with the £10m of additional funding provided to charities, wouldn't be visible to the naked eye on any graph with other government funding this year.

Of course, if governments across the world were told that 3% of their populations were at risk of suicide in the next 12 months, then the point of focus would, hopefully, shift. However, it is also worth noting that as this initial 3% lethality of COVID-19 figure has shifted, and as the proportion of the population susceptible figure has also shifted, little has changed in policy making thus far. For example, the famous "half a million deaths" forecast by Neil Ferguson's model was based on this 3% lethality and 100% of the population being susceptible; whereas, now, the lethality is estimated at 0.05% for under-70's, and 0.23% for the population at large.

Further, those susceptible is up for significant debate, with a series of studies suggesting that T-cell immunity could have been as high as 50% before the virus even arrived in the UK, and that, while antibodies appear to wane after a number of weeks, T-cell immunity could last for decades.

Some of you may have even seen the recent Spectator article that estimates the number of average lives that will be lost as a result of the economic downturn due to extreme measures equates to 560,000, which brings the tactic of lockdowns into question without even considering the mental health impact.

I raise these points for three reasons: the first is to present a balanced discussion; the second is that it might suggest that my initial assumption that if the data changed, the government might change its mind could be wrong -- although, it is worth noting that the data the government is seeing is not changing dramatically, with SAGE suggesting that 93% of the population is still susceptible; and the third is that to focus solely on the impacts of the measures imposed on mental health would be to fail to take into consideration the deeper impact of feeling those measures are unjustified and punitive, if found in the messy mêlée of confusing reporting, conspiracy theories on social media, errors in government data, and being lost on the side of the argument that is as equally unbalanced as the 'mainstream' media's side; it would be to neglect the deeper impact of feeling forgotten, the deeper impact of, not just the endless stream of negative news, but, worse, the feeling of being manipulated or lied to due to the lack of balanced discussion, or, equally, feeling as though you are not capable of discussing how you feel for fear of censure – I certainly know how deep an impact that final restriction can have, and much in the same way as how I have a right to be open about my sexuality without fear of discrimination, those who wish to raise an eyebrow at the government's handling of this pandemic with the view to having an open discussion have the right to do so without fear of being branded amoral, because the wider impacts on mental health do, in themselves, provide justified cause to raise that eyebrow.

The first of these wider impacts is what is being referred to as 'lockdown loneliness', which has been estimated to have affected 50% of 16–24-year-olds, and, as I have already explained the severe impact of loneliness in a recent piece (Thu Oct 22, 1:00pm -- should you wish to remind yourselves), I won't go into more detail on this; instead, I will simply refer you to the dataset compiled by the ONS.

The second impact worth pointing out is the prevalence of suicidal thoughts (a significant indicator of depression) that was estimated to be as high as 14% in 18–29-year-olds between March 31 and May 11 (the first lockdown) in a study conducted by University of Glasgow in conjunction with Samaritans.

The third impact of note has been the reduction in "coping mechanisms", whether that is face-to-face contact with friends, team sports (a point of particular note with children's grassroot activities being cancelled with this second lockdown), or work, another point of particular note with the numbers of young people losing their jobs continuing to rise.

Further, 43% of psychiatrists have seen an increase in urgent and emergency cases following the first COVID-19 lockdown. At the same time, 45% of psychiatrists have seen a fall in their most routine appointments, leading to fears of a 'tsunami' of mental illness after the pandemic, and the charity Mind has found that almost a quarter of people who tried to access mental health services during a fortnight in April failed to get any help.

These are not only just a small sample of the data available, a narrow snapshot of the far-reaching and wide-ranging impacts on mental health, but, as is the limit of data, also only look at the impact so far and do not consider the longer-term potential damage that psychiatrists are predicting. Although, perhaps calling for more models and projections after recent developments is not the answer.

In conclusion, with regards to mental health, while we are yet to know the full extent, and most likely won't for years, if not decades, to come, there are many aspects of the measures in place that are having impacts ranging from mild to severe that, in order to make informed decisions, ought to be considered in conjunction with the ambition of controlling the virus when evaluating the effectiveness of these measures.

Finally, although I cannot definitively conclude on whether these Lockdowns are "worthwhile", I do feel confident enough to conclude that, given the swathes of compelling evidence, it would be remiss to not include "lockdowns" as a bonus feature to the series of social causes of depression and anxiety, and so, once again, I will say, if you are feeling mentally affected by the introduction of Lockdown 2.0, you are not abnormal, and you are most certainly not alone.

End of Part Two

Part Three

The Lockdown Files

10 reasons to be anti-lockdown

25th December 2020

Published in Lockdown Sceptics 28th December 2020

1. **The research**: While those who oppose lockdowns have rigorously sought to justify their position with research -- and can reference tens of studies as to the lack of efficacy of lockdowns (or stringent measures under different names) -- the government has been capable only of publishing one graph in their "cost-benefit analysis" of the tiers which appeared to show a correlation between Tier 3 measures and a reduction in cases (since debunked).

2. **The use of data**: While those who oppose lockdowns have analysed all data in as close to real time as possible, the "data" used to justify lockdowns has been cherry-picked and often predictive, while being based on spurious assumptions that have repeatedly been proved inaccurate.

3. **The source and balance of information**: While those who oppose lockdowns possess no bias in obtaining their information, the government is informed on the risks by a number of committees (Sage, Nervtag, SPI-M) whose sole responsibility is to consider the virus and present the risks of that virus.

4. **The expertise of sources**: While those who oppose lockdowns have been *entertained* by commentators, cartoonists, comedians, and so on, they have been *informed* by scientists and medical professionals (Gupta, Heneghan, Spector, Yeadon, Craig, et al.). The government, however, has a disturbing proportion of *social* scientists or *behavioural* scientists (with no relevant expertise) informing each of their actions.

5. **The fear campaign**: While those who oppose lockdowns have sought to bring joy, maintain sanity, spread compassion, and care for people – all people, the government has operated a campaign of fear and propaganda unlike anything we have seen before in this country. Were this situation a severe threat to life, the message would undoubtably be one of "Keep Calm and Carry On"; there is a reason that the first piece of advice in any crisis is always to not panic: level-headedness leads to good decision making.

6. **The costs (part 1 -- health)**: While those who oppose lockdowns plead to the masses to understand how depression has tripled in 16-39 year olds this year, how still births have potentially quadrupled this year, how the largest underlying factor in deaths of those suffering with dementia or Alzheimer's (which

contributes to c.10% of deaths in the UK each year) is loneliness and that the treatment of the suffering elderly – stripping them of dignity, of compassion, of their grip on reality – has been a death sentence in and of itself, how domestic abuse has soared, and many other factors, the government appears blinkered to any health costs that are not Covid related.

7. **The costs (part 2 -- economy)**: While those who oppose lockdowns seek to understand the economic costs, and seem to understand that "economic" costs cannot simply be separated from health costs (killing small businesses kills livelihoods, drives up depression, drives up inequality – which has been shown to be *more* correlated with Covid-related deaths than the severity of lockdown measures), drives down tax revenues, drives down potential spending on healthcare, drives down life expectancy), the government seems content on prioritising health over economy (which doesn't make sense as explained) and throwing money at "economy" issues.

8. **The costs (part 3 -- culture)**: While those who oppose lockdowns seek to support the culture of this country – be that in supporting small businesses, art galleries, museums, music, pubs, or sport), the government seems content on the great erasure of what it means to be British.

9. **Censorship and debate**: While those who oppose lockdowns are constantly appealing for open debate and free speech, the government is avoiding open debate, seeking instead to censor dissenting voices. Further, as there is a push to censor any "misinformation", one can quite easily conclude that the *mass* information available, and uncensored, from dissenting voices must therefore be much closer to irrefutable having had to pass a much higher standard in order to simply be available.

10. **Motivation**: While those who oppose lockdowns have invested time and effort, the government has invested near on half a trillion pounds of the people's money in their "fight against the virus"; should that be proven to be a waste, they would lose power, they would lose credibility, they would lose everything. While those who oppose lockdowns and those who support lockdowns alike have been able to achieve some degree of fame and notoriety through positioning themselves centre-stage, those who oppose lockdowns have been subject to ridicule, defamation, slander, and abuse; they have risked their careers and reputations. They have done this for what they have believed is right and worth fighting for; they have done this to fight for each and every one of us; they have done this in the name of compassion.

Why is scepticism not growing?

30th December 2020

In all the polls I've seen in the last week or so, it appears that about 70% of the population will support a third national lockdown. It's a disturbingly high figure, and over the last couple of days, I have been questioning why this figure is so high.

Yes, the Government's nudge unit has appeared to have operated a skilful campaign in petrifying and muzzling the population; yes, the MSM have lapped up the Party line more enthusiastically than my brother's black Labrador attacks his water bowl after a long walk; and, yes, social media has, as always, been awash with the very vocal peddlers of the woke orthodoxy while dissenters are censored; but is this all? Is this enough to maintain support for the lockdowns at 70%?

You may, very reasonably, be thinking, *Yes, that's lots.* Fair enough.

However, I am reluctant to accept any explanation which is predicated on the assumption that the Government has been remotely competent in anything it has done with regards to dealing with Covid-19 – including drumming up and maintaining support for its nonsensical response to the virus. And so, I began to wonder if there isn't another explanation, one that is more deeply embedded in

Governmental incompetence than any planned action executed effectively.

And then it struck me, entirely out of the blue, as if it had been standing within 2m of me for more than fifteen minutes: What if the support for the Government's lockdowns is so widespread actually *because* of their incompetence?

Why is not everyone strongly opposed to lockdowns when it's documented how there is no correlation between lockdowns and Covid-19 deaths? Or when so many have lost their jobs, businesses, livelihoods? Or when the impacts on mental health are being felt by so many? Or when there are so many contradictions and errors and lies in what the Government has said? Or when the PCR tests are so unreliable that Covid-19 could be no more prevalent than any of the other endemic coronaviruses? Or when so many key parts of this discussion are simply not discussed – from Vitamin D, to HCQ, to cross-infection immunity, to asymptomatic transmission, to issues with the vaccine, and so on, and so on, almost ad infinitum.

One would, intuitively, with everything mentioned above, expect that lockdown scepticism should have an R-value that exceeds that of the virus; however, there are those who intuitively expect masks or lockdowns, as they are, to work, so let's park intuition for a moment, because the truth is that scepticism is not spreading as fast as it reasonably should and it's worth considering why this is.

I believe it is, counterintuitively, because there are so many elements to lockdown scepticism; if anything, by having such a compelling case made up of more strains of evidence than there are of Covid-19, it has reached a point where understanding the full picture requires hours of invested time, where having it all explained to a non-sceptic can leave that individual overwhelmed, potentially unable to take any of it in, especially when so many of those strains are directly linked to either Governmental incompetence, or poor reporting by the MSM, both of which the non-sceptic has trusted all year.

It is already known, not just from the complete disregard of all financial, health, or mental health consequences of the lockdowns, but also from reams of psychological study, that a non-sceptic, by virtue of being human, will struggle to hold more than one idea in their minds at any given point. Is it any wonder, therefore, that offering up multiple reasons, all contradicting their belief that the Government is competent and the MSM wouldn't lie to them, all at the same time, isn't having the desired effect?

Perhaps, unfortunately, it falls to us, the sceptics, to revise our strategy of spreading the good word.

Perhaps we should not bombard, berate, or ridicule the uninformed who appear to have conducted zero independent research. Yes, they probably deserve it;

but would it help? After all, those who remain non-sceptics have now had nine months of being brainwashed, have now become heavily invested in their way of thinking, and this cannot be undone with just one conversation.

The entire Covid-19 saga has been painfully polarising; they called us Covidiots, we called them Bedwetters; but, maybe, as those who will ultimately be on the right side of history, it falls to us to start bridging that gap? If for no other reason than this: I find myself worried about the non-sceptics – I imagine many of them are in desperate need of a good hug.

It waits for me

3rd January 2021

Published in Lockdown Sceptics 4th January 2021

It waits for me, 'round the corner;
It waits for me to be alone;
It waits for me, when we part ways;
It waits for me, it's there, I know.

I've faced it down from time to time,
I beat it once, twice, time again,
But it haunts me, still, ev'ry day,
And it's just a question of when.

When will I face this beast of mine?
When will it be at that corner
I turn; at that very next step?
When will it be all I have left?

When will it take me in its arms?
Embrace me, hold me, whisper to me
What I'd told myself already:
That tomorrow need not be.

It waits to be my only friend
By my side; all else shut inside,
Shut away, away from me, away
From seeing what might be my end.

It waits for me to be alone.
And it knows it won't need to wait
Much longer to truly have me
To itself.

But as I breathe, I know I must
Fight with all I am to conquer
This beast of mine, and his, and hers.
I'm not alone, I'm not deterred.

I'll wait for it, I'll face it down.
I'll wait for it, I'm not alone.
I'll wait for it, I'll stand and fight.
I'll wait for it, I'll win, I know.

The rise in depression is not something that will disappear when the lockdowns end

5ᵗʰ January 2021

"It is no measure of health to be well-adjusted to a sick society." – Jiddu Krishnamurti

In a recent piece (titled *Loneliness)* I explained the fundamentals of one of the major social causes of depression and anxiety, loneliness, and there are a number of others, but today I want to discuss brain functionality or formation, or genetic make-up, given how common a story it is to say that someone is depressed or anxious because their brain is "broken" in some way.

And this isn't just a common story told by the ill-informed, it is also a very common story told by medical professionals around the world, so it is worth paying some attention to.

A mental health problem that originates from an event is known as 'reactive', while a problem that has no event-based cause, (and is therefore believed to be the result of biology alone), is known as 'endogenous', (possibly because calling depression 'proactive' would be highly inappropriate). However, the medical professionals are wildly speculative about the prevalence of endogenous depression, with suggestions ranging from one in twenty cases to fewer than one in a hundred.

Nonetheless, there are still some interesting aspects around physiology that should be discussed, starting with brain functionality, because it is well documented that a brain scan of an individual suffering with depression or anxiety will look drastically different to the scan of a mentally 'healthy' individual. For example, in a depressed person, the areas that light up when we feel unhappy will be both larger and much more lit up than someone in a sound mental condition, and in a person suffering with anxiety, the areas that alert us to risk will be similarly inflated and illuminated.

This has been one of the justifications for the story that mentally ill people have "broken brains"; however, in recent times, it has become clear that our brains are constantly changing and adapting to the environments they are found in as well as being just as trainable as any muscle in the body and it does all this changing and adapting through two methods of synapse maintenance: the shedding of unwanted or unnecessary synapses; and the building up of regularly used synapses.

A great example of the former maintenance method is how any baby born anywhere in the world is born with the capability of speaking any language and it is only as they are brought up speaking just one (or more in the lucky case of multilingual people) that the synapses that would be needed to speak other languages are shed.

If you want an example of the latter maintenance method, then simply think of anything you have worked hard at and found becoming easier and easier over time; from meditation, to bicep curls.

In the case of depression, this 'maintenance' is still going on, only the brain has become slightly confused; as you spend longer and longer in a prolonged state of sadness and hopelessness, the brain begins to think that those synapses required to feel joy and pleasure are redundant and they start being shed, while those synapses that pick up on feelings of despair are built up and enhanced.

What this means is that even when the initial trauma or event that knocked you down has passed, the brain has become fixed in a state that prohibits you from recovering mentally. This is one of the reasons why so many people find it so difficult to "justify" their depression, struggling to identify a reason for why they feel quite as bad as they do – a struggle that creates a whole new layer of issues to battle with.

The second reason why people often find it difficult to put their finger on a justifiable cause for their stress is because we are told we need certain things to be happy and successful that simply aren't true. For example, I remember being told at school that I had no reason to be unhappy because I was receiving a great education, my family had money, and I was intelligent and had a bright future; that was apparently all that I should have wanted in life, and my need to not have to hide who I was and to be accepted was therefore a foolish notion.

What about genetics, then? How valid is the story that depression and anxiety are inherited? From personal experience, I've always believed that there must be a genetic factor: I know that there is a history of depression in my family -- my Grandma and I used to have long conversations about depression, and she was the first person I shared any writing I did on depression with.

There are two studies of note here, the first of which features in the Falk W Lohoff paper, Overview of the Genetics of Major Depressive Order (2010). The most common method of measuring how much of something is inherited is to compare non-identical twins with identical twins, (as identical twins share all the same genetics), and this is what Lohoff did to calculate that depression and anxiety are 37% inherited. Now, this may sound very high, and it is definitely significant, but also far too low to be deemed a cause. To put this 37% into context, height is 90% inherited.

Even as research has continued, no specific gene has been discovered that causes depression, meaning there is no one gene that if you don't have you won't ever become depressed; however, in a twenty-five year study conducted by Avshalom Caspi that mapped the genes of, and then followed, 1,000 babies in New Zealand up to adulthood, it was concluded that there is a particular variation of a gene called 5-HTT that does have a relationship with depression, and having this particular variation does greatly increase your chances of becoming depressed.

However, this is one of those genes that requires activation, and, in this case, that activation can be caused by a deeply stressful event, or a significantly traumatic childhood. Therefore, as is our best understanding today, one's sensitivity to depression can be increased by genes, but genes alone cannot cause depression.

If anyone thinks that the depression crisis we are seeing right now will be reversed when "this is all over", my conclusion to all of the above is that that simply cannot be true. Not only will the actions of Government have provided a sufficiently stressful event to have activated 5-HTT in so many of those who have it (something which cannot be deactivated), but the prolonged cycle of lockdowns will have extended for a sufficient length of time to allow for significant synapse maintenance, fixing in place a brain structure conducive to depression. And with mental health support from the NHS having been genuinely overwhelmed for years, I have no confidence in those needing support being able to get it on a timely basis.

I can only offer a small amount of consolation here. The philosopher Jiddu Krishnamurti said *"It is no measure of health to be well-adjusted to a sick society.* " But we can flip that on its head; there is no doubt that we are living through a period of society being very sick indeed, and, because of that, it is no mark of shame if you are finding yourself among the many who are struggling right now -- none whatsoever.

A Postcard of "long-Covid" from my sofa

11th January 2021

A week ago, I was struck down, and commenced my battle with, "Covid-19". Or, at least, three people I have come into "close-contact" with tested positive upon development of cold symptoms, among six of us developing cold symptoms that, while massively varied, all resembled those that are associated with The Great Plague.

As I am a healthy 25-year-old, I was desperately worried that this would present a significant issue at some point soon; after all, I'd had a surgery three years ago, after which my immune system had dipped; I had tonsilitis every other month for a couple of years until I drastically cut back on my smoking – possibly should have done this sooner. As such, it came as no surprise that my symptoms appeared to be the most severe of the six of us infected.

On the first day of my own personal war against this accursed virus, I had a splitting headache, chills, dizziness, a nasty cough, among other less discussable symptoms. My sense of smell disappeared; insofar as my nose was entirely blocked by this dreadful flu-like 'incapacitator'; and my sense of taste abandoned me; insofar as I was able to stomach a Domino's pizza – although that was all I ate that day, and it's hardly like I would have been able to identify any additional "gastrointestinal issues".

These symptoms faded over the course of the week and were replaced by an intense fatigue; so, naturally, as I didn't feel perfectly fine after seven days, I became utterly petrified that I would need to arm myself for the inevitable siege conducted by the forces of "long-Covid".

In order the quell the swelling of my Hancock-induced Munchausen's, I got online to quickly identify the symptoms I had that could be matched up with those listed on the NHS website as being associated with the perilous long-Covid.

Common long COVID symptoms include:

- *extreme tiredness (fatigue)*
- *shortness of breath*
- *chest pain or tightness*
- *problems with memory and concentration ("brain fog")*
- *difficulty sleeping (insomnia)*
- *heart palpitations*
- *dizziness*
- *pins and needles*
- *joint pain*
- *depression and anxiety*
- *tinnitus, earaches*
- *feeling sick, diarrhoea, stomach aches, loss of appetite*
- *a high temperature, cough, headaches, sore throat, changes to sense of smell or taste*
- *rashes*

Sure enough, I was able to tick off enough of these to confirm my self-diagnosis. In fact, if I thought carefully enough, I was able to tick them all off.

Happy with my diagnosis of long-Covid an entire week after first noticing symptoms, I allowed myself the luxury of some mindless web-browsing, and soon found myself on the NHS website page for Chronic Fatigue Syndrome/Myalgic Encephalomyelitis (CFS/ME); which not only suggested viral infections as a trigger, but also listed out the symptoms as follows:

The main symptom of CFS/ME is feeling extremely tired and generally unwell.

In addition, people with CFS/ME may have other symptoms, including:

- *sleep problems*
- *muscle or joint pain*
- *headaches*
- *a sore throat or sore glands that are not swollen*
- *problems thinking, remembering or concentrating*
- *flu-like symptoms*
- *feeling dizzy or sick*
- *fast or irregular heartbeats (heart palpitations)*

It struck me as odd that every symptom here could be found on the long-Covid symptoms page, but, resolute as I was in my self-diagnosis, I decided to filter out the symptoms that appeared on both pages to see clearly what was unique to my disease.

I then filtered out *changes to sense of smell or taste, shortness of breath, chest pain or tightness* as these were all Covid-19 symptoms anyway. I then filtered out *rashes*, because they could be anything, including spending more time on the sofa. I then filtered out *pins and needles* because I'm pretty convinced that we're all getting more pins and needles as a result of spending more time on the sofa. And finally, I filtered out *tinnitus, earaches* because, in my case at least, my earache was a result of a build-up of wax that happens whenever I get a cold.

This is what was left:

- *depression and anxiety*

I remembered that the NHS' CFS/ME page also said the following:

> *CFS/ME can affect anyone, including children. It's more common in women, and tends to develop between your mid-20s and mid-40s.*

I remembered the BBC reported a rise in depression in 16-39-year-olds from 11% to 31% in 2020.

I remembered that 20-44-year-olds account for about 21.5m people, or roughly a third of the population.

I realised that 0.31 x 0.33 ≈ 0.1; or, to put it another way: if the virus spreads indiscriminately, with each infection, there is a 1 in 10 chance it will infect someone between 20 and 44 who is currently suffering with depression.

Finally, I remembered that the ONS is claiming that 1 in 10 cases of Covid-19 progress into long-Covid.

It was at this point that I paused to think. I may not be considering like for like exactly, because I don't have perfect data to hand, but could it possibly be that long-Covid is in fact nothing new? That it is simply CFS/ME compounded by the depression that these lockdowns have created on a huge scale? Did the Government actually manage to create "long-Covid", not just as a propaganda tool for the summer months, nor just as an excuse for the rise in depression and anxiety their lockdowns created, but as a fully formed disease in its own right?

Questions for the PM and the Health Secretary

12th January 2021

Mr Johnson, Mr Hancock, as the mainstream media have failed drastically in doing their jobs, I have compiled here the questions that I, and many of my loved ones, would like to see you answer in one of those press conferences.

- Will you acknowledge and apologise for the pain, suffering, and harms your policies have caused?
- Will you acknowledge and apologise for the ruined lives of those whose businesses you have destroyed?
- Will you acknowledge and apologise to those in whom your policies have created mental health problems, eating disorders, fitness problems that will take years to overcome?
- Will you acknowledge and apologise for the lives cut short by suicide in 2020 when the data becomes available in September?
- Will you acknowledge and apologise for the claims people have made that suicides have not increased when you know full well that the data will not be available until September this year?
- Will you acknowledge that it was your restrictions that caused these deaths?

- Will you apologise to all those who have been trapped in their homes with abusive partners or parents?
- Will you acknowledge and apologise for the divisiveness your policies have created in our society?
- Will you acknowledge and apologise to all the children whose education has been catastrophically impacted?
- Will you acknowledge and apologise for the massive increase in inequality your policies have created?
- Will you acknowledge and apologise to those who will have had their lives cut short or irreparably damaged by being unable to receive basic healthcare?
- Will you acknowledge and apologise to those who will be living and dying of cancer because of missed diagnoses as a result of your policies?
- Will you acknowledge and apologise to those who will suffer from hypochondriac conditions as a result of your repeated message to act as if diseased when in fact entirely healthy?
- Will you acknowledge and apologise to the developing and now struggling economies that depend on British tourism?
- Will you acknowledge and apologise to all the disabled individuals who have been attacked and discriminated against because of your policies?
- Will you apologise to the youth of our country who have been vilified in the name of your campaign of fear?

- Will you acknowledge and apologise for the blood that is on your hands?

Thanks,

Jonny

Let's turn the questions back on the lockdown proponents

30th January 2021

Too often the lockdown proponents ask the question, "Well, what's the alternative?" Or they state, "This is the only way to save lives." They should neither be making blanket statements, nor requiring the opposers to come up with alternatives. This is just completely backwards. Everyone should be asking questions of them, and I have a few here.

What happens if a third of NHS staff, most of whom are fit and healthy, don't come in to work?

What happens when those who are in work have to pick up the workload of those not in work, while a nasty winter season is going on, while having to spend hours faffing with PPE each week?

What happens if we remove 13,000 beds from our hospital capacity to accommodate for social distancing?

What happens when the hospitals use a traffic light system that backs up the emergency departments?

What happens when Covid symptom-free individuals who are sick enough to be in hospital get a false positive test and are automatically then placed on a ward where SARS-CoV-2 abounds?

What happens when ambulances have to queue up outside hospitals because of backed up emergency departments, leaving individuals sick enough to require an ambulance and emergency care waiting for everyone in front to get a covid-test?

What happens when this means there are no ambulances free to pick up the woman having a stroke five minutes down the road?

What happens when the man having a heart attack is too scared to come into hospital for fear of catching a virus?

What happens over the next few years with all the people who missed diagnoses or treatments this past year?

What happens over the next few decades while tax revenue is down, and budget cuts are made on the NHS when the past year showed us all how woefully underfunded it already was?

What happens to people's immune systems when they're forced to stay indoors and exercise less?

What happens when incomes go down, nutritional quality goes down, stress goes up, and substance abuse goes up? Do obesity or substance abuse related conditions not already make up a phenomenal cost to the NHS?

What happens when a small business collapses, and that family ceases being able to cope or hold onto any sense of a hopeful future? Are the mental health services in the NHS not already a constantly and significantly overwhelmed part of the NHS?

What happens when our children's developments are suspended for a year?

What happens when our children stop being able to see any point in exerting any effort?

There are so many more that could be asked here, but I will just ask three more:

1. What is the total cost, to life itself and otherwise, of all of these facets of lockdowns?
2. If none of these had happened, if instead we had asked those who felt sick to stay home, and offered them financial support, and if we had offered financial support to the elderly and vulnerable to stay home should they wish, how many more would have died at the hands of the virus?
3. Which of those two numbers is higher?

I know which I think it is. It kind of seems like a no-brainer to me. But crucially, with each day that passes, the costs in question 1 are mounting while the risks associated with switching to the approach outlined in question 2 are diminishing.

With each day that passes, staying in lockdown becomes more and more monumentally misguided.

Queer culture

31ˢᵗ January 2021

I think this piece deserves a proper foreword, because there's some drama here that needs to be unpacked.

Almost annoyingly, once unpacked, it's much less dramatic, but this is the story:

This was a piece written for work (and should perhaps have been included in Part Two, but I decided chronology was more important, so here we are), upon request, which initially seemed troublesome, what with my belief that my employer at the time was already too far down the rabbit hole of woke-ism to be saved, and with my belief that the only thing I cared about now was making sure these restrictions ended and were never to be brought back again.

I mean, what value is there in culture when there is nowhere you can experience that culture?

But I tackled the assignment and produced what is below, except for the opening paragraph which was added later.

I sent it in on Monday 1ˢᵗ February 2021 only to hear nothing for a week.

I sent a chaser Monday 8ᵗʰ February 2021 only to hear that it was with the comms and compliance team, or something, and that it was having to go through checks.

Now, that was the response I got to asking what the person I'd emailed it to directly had thought of it.

Hardly a glowing review.

As you may be thinking as you read this, I had assumed that I was being censored for expressing already drastically self-censored and moderated anti-lockdown views.

As it turned out, this was not the case.

After a lengthy call on the 12th February, it became clear that the comms guy had an issue with my use of the word "queer".

Needless to say, we had a bit of a laugh at home about the ridiculousness of this.

Censor my anti-lockdown views, by all means, it's undermining democracy, but it's happening everywhere, so fine, but if you are so worried about identity politics and being perceived to use a word that might be offensive to the outside world that you will censor one of your own staff using the term by which they "identify" then surely you have to question your own hypocrisy and superficiality?

I popped "identify" in speech marks above because I loathe the word. I don't identify as anything. I relate to certain things; I feel comfortable in certain settings; I have an identity, of which being queer is a part; but being queer is not my identity.

It's semantics and nomenclature, sure, but it matters to me – and yes, I do see the irony in being precious about not wanting to be seen as "identifying" as anything.

Anyway… rather than kick up a massive fuss over this, I added an extra paragraph, the opening paragraph, which, now you know the story, may be more entertaining than it was for those who read it blind.

When I received the "final version with just a couple of edits", I decided to run a document compare to see what they'd taken out. These have been identified below in italics.

I can fully appreciate removing "G-A-Y" – it's a private company/brand, and it's understandable that they would wish to disassociate themselves from an external brand.

I am frustrated by the censoring of my comparison between the removal of freedoms within the AIDS crisis and the Lockdown crisis. I would have been able to understand had they removed a couple of the more inflammatory words; for example, editing "this Government degradingly removed, by diktat, our freedom to choose when and with whom we have sex*" to "*this Government removed our freedom to choose…*"

Removing a reference to the AIDS crisis because it mentions *the Government is bordering on the ridiculous when I'd been tasked with writing a piece for "LGBT History Month".*

But to remove my pay-off line because it's too sexual... *The final sentence is not simply thrown in to give readers a laugh, but also to sum up what "queer culture" is for me, what it is I can't wait to get back, and puritanically removing it is so disappointing.*

That said... this is still a piece that goes, in large part, against identity politics, and against lockdowns. So, the fact it was published at all should give us hope!

Having titled this piece "Queer Culture", I feel it is important to note at this point that I use the word "queer" both carefully, and specifically, as it encapsulates not only how I personally feel about myself, but also the general identity of my little subsection of the overarching LGBTQ+ umbrella, while having none of the negative connotations that "gay" always had as I was growing up. "Queer" is my word, and I own it with pride. I point this out not only to give you a little more flavour of the position from which I write, but also to highlight an idea that will be explored in more depth later on: that there is no such single identity as LGBTQ+; there is far more nuance to it than that.

I wrote a piece for the Gatwick office a while back now on loneliness, and the devastating effects it has; among them, that acute loneliness produces the same cortisol levels as being attacked by a stranger, and that it is as deadly as obesity. In this piece I explained how one can be lonely in specific ways, while being socially replete in all other ways; and the example I gave was that I could have people lining up round the corner to join me at cricket matches (when that "luxury" is made available to us again), while also feeling that I have no "queer community", and that I could therefore feel lonely in one respect, while feeling socially satiated in all others.

But, while I feel like I have been deeply lacking in queer culture, it is important to ask what on earth that is. I am acutely aware that the scenes I used to frequent in Soho and the rest of central London were heavily geared toward the distinctly white gay community. I am also very aware of the fact that what I would consider a home-from-home would be somewhere that might be considered unwelcoming to large swathes of the LGBT community. (Of course, one of the other predominant ways in which I derive a sense of "queer community" is through intimacy with another individual, but perhaps that is not one to explore much further.)

All of this begs the question, is there such a thing as queer culture? Can the customs, ideas, and social behaviour of Ballroom be likened to the Stonewall riots, for example? Can the arts and other collective manifestations that stem from the drag community even be compared to the overwhelmingly twink-focused nightlife scene of London's gay district?

I don't believe it's possible to neatly define queer culture, or queer community, when the individuals who make up this "community" are so widely diverse themselves, when the tastes and interests of a British Indian bisexual trans woman might have zero crossover with that of a gay white man.

This, I propose, is because of history. "Culture" can loosely be defined as the social behaviours and norms of a group established in that group's history, and the history of the gay community in the UK bears little resemblance to trans history, or black history, or even US specific gay history; even so, there is certainly a considerable amount of UK specific gay history that can be tracked in a neat timeline over the past 54 years.

From the Sexual Offences Act decriminalisation of sex between two men ("in private") in 1967, to the first London Pride march in 1972, to Terry Higgins dying of an AIDS-related illness in 1982 which drove homosexuality back to peak stigmatisation, to Thatcher's Section 28 of the Local Government Act in 1988 that effectively banned tackling homophobia in schools, to the WHO finally removing homosexuality as a mental illness in 1992, to the Admiral Duncan in Soho in 1999, through to same-sex marriages being legalized in 2014.

But what, in terms of gay history in the UK, has happened since then? What was there left to fight for? Greater visibility, deeper social acceptance? Sure. But was there anything historic? I would argue not.

Is it important that no child feels afraid to be open with their friends and family? Vitally so, yes. But this is not something that can be won in some landmark case in the courts; this is something that will develop over time in line with national cultural progression, and it is something that is happening, with homophobic slurs being simultaneously phased out while also becoming verboten, and with homophobic bullying becoming less commonplace than social ostracization for being homophobic. Of course, some middle ground, where open debate and the sharing of beliefs and ideologies is welcomed would be preferable, but that is most likely an issue for another day.

So, what exactly is this sense of having no "queer community" that contributes heavily to the toxic feeling of loneliness I feel so often?

It is, as loneliness is, at once a personal matter and a community matter. I have my personal ways, specific to me, of fostering a feeling of belonging, and since *the day this Government degradingly removed, by diktat, our freedom to choose when and with whom we have sex, a freedom, it should be noted, not removed in the height of the AIDS crisis when assessing the risks was left to the individual,* and since bars and clubs have been shut, I have had none of the means by which I derive that sense of community available to me.

We can debate the necessity and efficacy of that removal of freedoms, but one thing is known: freedoms curtailed are never so easily reclaimed, and it is becoming increasingly clear that the cultures we once knew and loved, in whatever form they took, *from the drag scene to G-A-Y*, will not be returned to us with the flicking of a switch come the day it is deemed 'safe'.

But there is one element of queer culture that exists in all walks of the LGBTQ+ community, and across all branches of LGBTQ+ history, and that is fighting for our rights, fighting for our freedoms. And it seems now that there may come a day in the not too distant future where all those who fall under the diverse umbrella that is "LGBTQ+" will need to set an example, will need to make proud those who fought so we could have the freedoms we do, and will need to step up once more to reclaim what was lost a year ago, because I, for one, do not want to wait a day longer than is necessary *to be surrounded by cute, slightly sweaty, slightly intoxicated young men in a slightly seedy London club.*

Let me be free

6th February 2021

Published in Lockdown Sceptics 7th February 2021

I don't want to see another masked human being.
I'd much rather smile and see others' feelings.

I don't want to hide, to cower and shelter.
I'd much rather greet, hug, and gather together.

I don't want to tune in to Zoom for my work,
Buffering, breaking, and all else that irks.

I'd much rather see all my colleagues in person
Than turn on my camera like some Orwellian
   classroom.

I don't want to spend e'en a single day more
Bat in my hand hitting balls at the wall.

I'd much rather be down at one end of a net
With a friend, or a foe, or a guy I just met.

I don't want to *ever* be socially distanced
At a gig, or a game, in the pub, or in romance.

I want to be close, to be loved, be connected,
Not bubbled, not spaced, not apart, nor 'protected'.

I want to be trusted to make my decisions,
A part of society not rife with division.

I want to be free, know my life is my own,
I'm done with this nonsense and with being alone.

I just want to be happy, to dance and be merry,
Not locked in my home, anxious and wary.

All that I want is a chance to be me,
With my place in the world, just let me be free.

In What Can I Hope?

11th February 2021

Published in Lockdown Sceptics 13th February 2021

With all this talk of 'horizon' and 'hope',
I wonder sometimes, 'Did I miss the boat?'
What is it that has these people excited?
Should I see it? Or have I been blinded?
Whatever it is, whatever they see,
Whatever they think, I know they're not me.
They'll never know what it is that I fear,
They'll never risk losing all I hold dear,
They'll never perceive the world through my eyes,
They'll never just sit at their desks and cry.

I envy them this, their blindness, their bliss,
Their freedom in hope, their faith in a wish.
I'd trade all I have for that faith and hope,
I'd give it away to look forward and know,
Know that tomorrow brings a brand-new day,
Know that tomorrow brings light, paves a way;
Paves a way, to joy, to reason, to worth,
To happiness, cheer, merriment, and mirth.
I envy their hope that all will be well,
But their hope alone does nothing to quell
My fears that I'll be left nought but a shell,
Left here on my own, in my fears to dwell.

For my fears pave my way, keep me this way,
Keep me locked up, hidden, keep me dismayed.
I see no reason to hold onto hope,
I see no reason to look forward and know

That all will be better. How can that be so
When, time after time, I've nothing to show.
I'm down a job, a house, a lover, and friends,
I know I've support, but when does this end?
When can I look to, in what can I hope,
When all I see makes it harder to cope.

A Red List Analysis

12th February 2021

Published in Lockdown Sceptics 15th February 2021

With hotel quarantine coming into effect on Monday, I think it's time we did some armchair sleuthing into the countries on our red list, because when I saw the list, it struck me, on first impression, as a broadly random selection of countries that, if anything, seemed more anti-African and anti-South American than anything else.

Of course, South Africa and Brazil featured in there because of the two now world-renowned "variants of concern" named after those countries, 501Y.V2 (of which, the UK has more cases than all other countries combined bar South Africa), and P.1 respectively.

Other than these two "VOCs", it is difficult to see what explanation could be offered for adding other countries to the red list, (seeing as there are no other major nationally branded "VOCs"), other than their case rates rising rapidly, or holding at a very high rate.

The explanation often cited is that we are defending our borders against as of yet unknown variants, but, if that is truly the case, then why highlight individual countries and not just shut our borders to everyone? Are some countries more likely to create "VOCs" than others? If so, why is that? I'm not sure that's a line of questioning anyone on SAGE would be happy to be taken down…

Perhaps it is a case of restricting travel from countries around SA and Brazil? There's an argument to be made here, with every country on mainland South America on the red list, along with Panama which shares a border with Colombia, but, if that were the case, why not Trinidad and Tobago, or Curacao, or Aruba, or Grenada, and so on and so on.

Of course, you also have all countries south of DRC on the list. But, why on earth would you add Mauritius before adding Madagascar? Or Seychelles, or Cape Verde? These seem more like holiday destinations the Government is seeking to dissuade travel to than genuine viral or variant threats.

So, other than broadly being countries near SA or Brazil, it must be the case rates adding to the decision process too then. So, let's take a look at those. But, before we do, maybe it would be helpful to have the list of 33 countries to hand:

Angola, Argentina, Bolivia, Botswana, Brazil, Burundi, Cape Verde, Chile, Colombia, Democratic Republic of the Congo, Ecuador, Eswatini, French Guiana, Guyana, Lesotho, Malawi, Mauritius, Mozambique, Namibia, Panama, Paraguay, Peru, Portugal (including Madeira and the Azores), Rwanda, Seychelles, South Africa, Suriname, Tanzania, United Arab Emirates (UAE), Uruguay, Venezuela, Zambia, Zimbabwe

Let's start with the ludicrous: four of these countries (French Guiana, Mauritius, Tanzania, and Zimbabwe) recorded no cases on February 11th. None. It is, however, worth noting that Tanzania haven't recorded a single case since May 8th when their Matt Hancock equivalent was sacked after a positive test being obtained from a papaya.

Another 14 countries have case rates per million in double figures. These are Angola, Burundi, DR of Congo, Lesotho, Rwanda, Malawi, Venezuela, Mozambique, South Africa – yes, South Africa, that terrifying country that is rife with mutant variants; Namibia, Suriname, Eswatini, Guyana, and Zambia. The highest of these is 56 cases per million.

For reference, the UK, despite having fallen by 80% since the peak of daily reported cases on the 8th January, sits at 199 cases per million.

And sure enough, another 9 of our 33 red listed countries, while having triple-figure case rates still have lower case rates than us. These 9 are Cape Verde, Bolivia, Ecuador, Colombia, Uruguay, Paraguay, Argentina, Panama, and Chile. Have we missed any South American or southern African countries?

Oh yes, of course, Brazil, home to VOC P.1, Peru, home to a potentially worse lockdown than ours, Botswana and Seychelles.

Let's look at these in more detail.

Peru

Cases reported 11th February: *6,724*

Case rate per million: *204*

Trend: *Seems to be reaching a peak, but the cases curve looks different to any other I've seen.*

Variants of concern: *Indeterminable from my armchair.*

Conclusion: *If you're applying the precautionary principle, here seems fairly reasonable, I suppose.*

Botswana

Cases reported 11th February: *491*

Case rate per million: *209*

Trend: *Nothing has really changed since the middle of October.*

Conclusion: *What on earth is happening in Botswana? Why has nothing changed for 4 months? That seems very weird. Yes, let's keep them out. Thanks.*

Brazil

Cases reported 11th February: *54,742*

Cases per million: *258*

Trend: *Broadly unchanged since early January.*

Trend of neighbouring countries: *Argentina has fallen 47% since peak on 12th January; Panama has fallen 84% since peak on 6th January; Colombia has fallen 63% since peak on 14th January; Bolivia has fallen 53% since peak on 27th January; Suriname has fallen 77% since peak on 12th January; Uruguay down 63% since peak 14th January; Venezuela has been low since mid-October; Paraguay has been broadly unchanged since September; Guyana low*

since August; Ecuador hasn't really changed since
April.
Conclusion: *There just doesn't appear to be a hugely*
concerning variant of concern ripping through South
America right now...

Seychelles
Cases reported 11th February: *73*
Cases per million: *745*
Trend: *Cases appear to be growing*
Conclusion: *Surely having a sample size of less than*
100,000 (i.e. their entire population) means that
cases per million will just be distorted. I'm not sure
a comparison here is worthwhile at all.

We have two countries left on our list: Sir Charles
Walker MP's highly referenced (as he calls Matt
Hancock and his ideas out for what they are)
Portugal; and UAE; the only two countries not in
either Africa or South America. With cases per
million of 341 and 356 respectively, you could
almost accept these two being on the red list, but
really, Portugal has seen a decline of 79% daily cases
reported since its peak on January 28th, and UAE
appears to have peaked on January 29th, although it
isn't coming down as quickly as some other countries
on this list.

If I were to speculate as to how the Government had
come up with this list, I would say that it seems to me
that the Government has had someone draw a big
circle around Brazil and South Africa on a big map,
and they've thrown those countries onto this red list,
without bothering to consider the fact that South

Africa is seeing a rapid decline in cases that exceeds even ours.

However, the map wasn't quite big enough and they forgot all the little countries around the north coast of Venezuela. They also, somehow forgot Madagascar.

Then, they did a quick google search for high cases per million which spat out Seychelles, Portugal, and UAE, so they added them to the list without even bothering to look at the fact that Portugal's cases are plummeting at the same rate as ours, UAE's cases are coming down fairly quickly, and Seychelles cases per million is simply an artefact of having such a small population.

All in all, I would struggle to conclude that this red list is a carefully thought out, carefully planned, carefully investigated plan that lists all high-risk countries. But then, I'm just armchair sleuthing, aren't I.

The Great Escape

13ʰ February 2021

Published in Lockdown Sceptics 14ᵗʰ February 2021

What follows here is an explanation of how I've created a legal excuse to get out of the country and find myself sitting on South Beach in Miami in two weeks' time; however, in doing so, I'm pretty sure there are a bunch of rules that I may have broken.

These breaches are, in my opinion though, harmless, necessary, and easy to get away with. Harmless because we know that travel contributes to such a small proportion of transmissions, but also because I have already had COVID and recovered, so I believe my travel is even more harmless than harmless. Necessary because I don't think I'll make it through to the next Great Goalpost Shift, whenever that is, without getting away for a bit. And easy to get away with because I've had some excellent help from complete strangers.

My first problem that needed overcoming was creating a legitimate and legal excuse for leaving the country. There seems to be a bit of hubbub around traveling for property viewing, but I decided the safest option was traveling for work. Of course, I want a break from everything, so I don't want to actually do any work when I could be sitting on a beach in 30-degree sun; and, regardless, my firm certainly wouldn't be sending me abroad any time soon when we are not even meant to be going into our own offices.

So I came up with a different idea. Here is the email I sent to a number of bars and pubs in Florida:

Hi [insert bar name],

I hope all is well with you.

I'm emailing from London, UK with a plea. As you may well know, we here in the UK are living under the cruel dictatorship of an unelected pseudo-Government called SAGE, the priests of the new religion that is stampeding across our now-God-forsaken country of worshipping the NHS. They have systematically removed every single part of life that makes life worth living, and, put simply, I'm not sure I will make it through the next few weeks — let alone the months that we are now being told we will have to endure.

What makes it all so much worse is that we are not only trapped in our houses, but we are now trapped on this island too, with only one means of escape: we can travel for work.

So, this is my plea to you: can I have a job interview?

It can be for anything — I'd happily take 1 shift a week cleaning floors on my hands and knees as a volunteer if it meant I could travel to one of the only places that has any right to call itself a "land of the free".

To be perfectly honest, it can even be a job interview where we both know I won't actually get a job; so long as you "insist" that the "interview" is face-to-face, I can show that to anyone who questions my travelling as proof that I am travelling for work.

I have a few things to wrap up here first, but I will be "free" to travel on the 25th Feb, so anything between the 26th-28th would work.

I hope this email falls on compassionate ears.

Kind regards,
J

One response was all I needed, and boy did I get one:

Hi J,

Thank you for your application for the role of bar staff.

We have had a large number of applications for this position, so it's with great joy that I am able to invite you for an interview for the position.

Here at [redacted bar name] we have a strong family ethos and so it is vitally important that we meet everyone who we might offer a job to in order to ensure that they will be a good fit for us.

With that in mind, would you be able to come down at 2pm Sunday 28th February?

Your interview would be largely informal, but we would like you to prepare a couple of cocktails, which we would then enjoy while having a chat to get to know you better!

Please let me know as soon as possible as there are many others who are keen for this role.

Best wishes,
C

I have now saved that email, but I am tempted to print it and frame it, or at the very least, laminate it before flying.

I then set my attentions on the ESTA. If my Government believed I was traveling for work, could I legitimately apply for a travel and tourism visa from the Department of Homeland Security? Answer: yes. I would book return flights, travel out there for the interview during which I would, of course, earn no money, but the trip could still be considered a legitimate work reason.

Sure enough, my ESTA was approved in under an hour, which meant I could book my flights. I'm sure it will come as no surprise that the outbound flight cost more than twice as much as the return flight – after all, what demand is there for flying into London right now?

However, even with a legitimate reason to travel, an approved ESTA, and booked flights, one issue remains. Ensuring I receive a negative COVID test within the three days before flying, especially as I had the damned thing only a month ago and we all know how long after recovering it is possible to show up as positive. That said, as I have three days, I can get in a fair few tests if I need to in order to ensure a genuine negative result.

So, that's that. I will be flying out in a couple of weeks and will then spend two weeks on the beach, in the sea, in the gym, in bars, pubs, and clubs, going on dates, reading in the sun, and generally just being with people.

I will be sure to send you a postcard from the Sunshine State!

The One Who Couldn't Actually Get Away

15th February 2021

I'm afraid I have to give you a very upsetting update having had a certain Biden proclamation pointed out to me.

The key section reads as follows:

Section 1. Suspension and Limitation on Entry. (a) The entry into the United States, as immigrants or nonimmigrants, of noncitizens who were physically present within the Schengen Area, the United Kingdom (excluding overseas territories outside of Europe), the Republic of Ireland, and the Federative Republic of Brazil during the 14-day period preceding their entry or attempted entry into the United States, is hereby suspended and limited subject to section 2 of this proclamation.

I did, however, wonder if there was anything under section 2 that could even vaguely be stretched to the point of relevance, and two possibilities jumped out at me:

(b) Section 1 of this proclamation shall not apply to: […]

(xii) any noncitizen whose entry would be in the national interest, as determined by the Secretary of State, the Secretary of Homeland Security, or their designees.

Given that I am an exceedingly entertaining fellow, I do believe it is in the national interest of the United States of America to have me in their country. However, I do not believe that the Secretary of State, the Secretary of Homeland Security, or their designees would be quite so easily persuaded.

Which brings me to the second possibility:

(b) Nothing in this proclamation shall be construed to affect any individual's eligibility for asylum, withholding of removal, or protection under the regulations issued pursuant to the legislation implementing the Convention Against Torture and Other Cruel, Inhuman or Degrading Treatment or Punishment, consistent with the laws and regulations of the United States.

I would, at this point, like to draw your attention to this Convention.

Once there, you will not need to look any further than Part 1, Article 1, which reads as follows:

PART I

Article 1

*1. For the purposes of this Convention, the term "torture" means any act by which severe pain or suffering, whether physical or mental, is intentionally inflicted on a person for such purposes as [...] intimidating or coercing him or a third person, or for any reason based on discrimination of any kind, when such pain or suffering is **inflicted by*** *or at the instigation of or with the consent or acquiescence of a public official* or other person acting in an official capacity. It does not include pain or suffering arising only from, inherent in or incidental to lawful sanctions.

2. This article is without prejudice to any international instrument or national legislation which does or may contain provisions of wider application.

My reading of this? My mental suffering (and many, many others') over the last year has been intentionally inflicted for the purposes of intimidating and coercing the population into compliance with the very regulations that are causing the mental suffering; the suffering has been inflicted at the instigation of The Quad (and especially the prime psychopath Matt Hancock), and the fact that this article is without prejudice to any national legislation, even such that seeks to limit the risk of the NHS being overwhelmed means that that is simply not a good enough excuse.

I would therefore conclude that we who are locked up with the boot on our necks should very much be eligible for asylum.

That said... I still don't think that this line would work. So, without further delay, I will get back in my box and get back to praying that I will be able to make it through the next few weeks.

Opportunity, Incentive, and Rationalisation

18th February 2021

Published in Lockdown Sceptics 21st February 2021

The question most often posed of me when I embark on yet another monologue about the endless lunacies plaguing our lives right now is 'why'; if what you're saying is true, if the damage is so great, if the virus isn't such a threat, if the efficacy of the measures is so low, then why would the Government be doing this to us?

We've heard a lot of discussion around 'cock-up', 'conspiracy', and even 'cockupspiracy'; be that, in the case of 'cock-up', the recurring inadequacy of advisors and politicians, in the case of 'conspiracy', more often than not, the Great Reset, and in the case of 'cockupspiracy', the opportunism of the likes of big tech and big pharma.

All of these are important factors that require attention; however, it seems to me that the debate has largely been based on the fallacy that the reason for all this lies somewhere on a spectrum between 'cock-up' and 'conspiracy', with 'cockupspiracy' falling somewhere in the centre. I do not believe this is the case, because I do not believe that there is a spectrum here.

What we are seeing, I'm sure many of you will agree, is a fraud – a wrongful or criminal deception intended to result in financial or personal gain (or avoidance of loss) – on a monumental scale, and, as such, and given my background in audit, I believe that, instead, this should be analysed with reference to the fraud triangle (below).

The fraud triangle (comprised of Opportunity, Rationalisation, and Incentive/Pressure) is the basic framework used to explain the reason behind an individual's decision to commit fraud, and so it is also going to be the basic framework by which I attempt to explain the Government's actions termed Polis-20 in James Alexander's piece in Lockdown Sceptics, *A Cockupspricacy (9th December 2020).*

Opportunity

"The pandemic represents a rare but narrow window of opportunity to reflect, reimagine, and reset our world" – Professor Klaus Schwab

"We couldn't get away with it in Europe, we thought... and then Italy did it. And we realised we could." – Neil Ferguson

If neither of these quotes sends shivers down your spine, then I can only conclude you are as spineless as our current leader.

I include these not because I believe that the Great Reset is the factor driving the pandemic response, or that Neil Ferguson is some criminal mastermind intent on watching the world burn, but because they highlight a key fundamental of my explanation: when people panic in the face of an unknown, they are more malleable; and when people are malleable, opportunities arise.

When the Government set about its plan of "three weeks to flatten the curve" – the one-year anniversary of which I am very excited to celebrate soon – it did so in the height of panic, with the desire to be seen to be doing "something", and in the face of mounting cries from the media of, "they're doing it, they're doing it, why aren't we doing it too?"

The Government, almost (but not quite) forgivably so, buckled under these conditions, and, as this was a reaction, this is not where the fraud was committed;

it is all that came after, once it became clear that what they had done had been a mistake, that constitutes the fraud, the wrongful or criminal deception intended to result in financial or personal gain.

The wrongful deception has been that the prolonging of lockdowns, the wearing of masks, the crippling of the economy, the devastation of our young, the destruction of our society and culture has all been not only necessary, but effective and worthwhile.

The financial or personal gain has been, among other factors that will be explored in the next section on Incentive/Pressure, that they would get away with the initial mistake.

The cruelty of the situation is that the observable evidence from the initial mistake, being the compliance, the willingness, and the acceptance, shows that the opportunity to get away with it lies not in walking away, but in doubling down on this initial mistake.

Incentive/Pressure

Before continuing, it is important to note that you will find some fraud triangles that specify Incentive as the third point, and some that specify Pressure. I will include both, because I can't see how they're interchangeable, and because they are both very important.

More often than not, when considering fraud, the gain in itself is the Incentive. A thief steals for the purpose of obtaining the thing it is they steal. However, in this case, the incentives are far reaching and widely varied.

We could discuss, for example, the PPE contract issued to a friend of Hancock's; we could discuss the shares in big pharma held by many members of Sage; we could discuss the fifty new billionaires who are all doctors, scientists, or healthcare entrepreneurs who would see their new-found lucrative TV deals dry up with the ending of this "public health crisis"; we could discuss the huge sums of advertising money the media have gained from the Government; we could discuss how profit-oriented big corporations are seeing their competition evaporate as their profits soar; we could discuss how the WEF, XR, BLM, and the CCP are committed to replacing capitalism (albeit in different ways); however, none of these are incentives for the Government so much as they are external pressures, external pressures to perpetuate the problem we find ourselves in.

Further to the external pressures, there are a number of internal pressures, mostly arising from those in Government who are quite clearly enjoying the heightened levels of importance and power. Lord Acton said it best when he penned a letter to Bishop Mandell Creighton in 1887, "Power tends to corrupt, and absolute power corrupts absolutely. Great men are almost always bad men."

But the fraud I'm discussing here is our Government attempting to weasel their way out of a catastrophic mistake, and the incentive I want to highlight is this: the cost of this mistake is dumbfounding; not just financially, but in so many other ways, and to such an extent that failing to get away with this mistake would inevitably lead to the collapse of governments globally, the ending of careers, and, more likely than not, significant prison sentences.

Rationalisation

The final point to the fraud triangle is Rationalisation, and, accepting the assumption that there are those in the Cabinet who aren't entirely psychopathic and lacking in human emotions, (although I would forgive you should you decide not to accept this assumption), it is the final part required to explain the reason behind this great fraud.

But there are two lines of thinking worth considering here. The first is that after a year of lies, gaslighting, and manipulation, the Government has come to believe their own deception, deluding themselves that now following an apparent strategy of ZeroCovid is indeed a strategy worth following; that this would be the strategy that would save the most lives.

However, with all the data available, this feels unlikely; given that a 'data not dates' approach should more closely resemble an immediate releasing of restrictions, coupled with a sincere apology, than a roadmap to freedom that involves a lack of freedoms extending for much longer, I am not convinced by this line of thinking.

The other line of thinking is that they are aware of the fear they have caused, they are aware of the pain and suffering they have caused, and they are, at least to some degree, aware of the pointlessness of it all; and, as a result, they are equally aware that an immediate releasing of restrictions, coupled with a sincere apology, would likely lead to a level of confusion and fury that could lead to severe civil unrest perhaps manifesting in riots and the unravelling of law and order.

The Rationalisation, therefore, is that the cost of honesty at this point could legitimately outweigh the severe costs they are aware the lockdowns and other restrictions cause.

I, personally, do not see this risk, or potential cost, as a likely outcome of well-managed honesty; but then, I believe I have more faith in my fellow Brits than the Government who has infantilised and demeaned their population for a year now clearly does.

I will leave you with one final thought, in case you believe that I am being overly cynical, or that the Government surely couldn't be doing what I am suggesting here: can you, in all honesty, tell me that better men have not done much worse for much less?

Level of population immunity in the UK

19th February 2021

Published in Lockdown Sceptics 20th February 2021

Here follows a Sage-styled parody paper.

Introduction and assumptions

The most important piece of information with regards to our position on the timeline of the pandemic is our proximity to the point defined as herd immunity – the point at which it is no longer possible for cases to rise exponentially.

In order to assess this, a number of factors need to be taken into consideration, and a number of assumptions need to be made.

For the purposes of this paper, it will be assumed that the NPIs have been 100% effective in protecting the elderly and vulnerable, and therefore, there will be no crossover between those who have had prior infection, and therefore obtained assumed immunity to the virus, and those who have received the vaccine, for which, it will be assumed, 80% immunity will be obtained upon receipt of the first dose and 90% immunity obtained upon receipt of the second dose.

In order to better assess the data, it will be assumed that "80% immunity" will mean 100% immunity in

80% of those administered the first dose of the vaccine.

While the WHO and the Stanford paper by John Ioannidis estimate the Infection Fatality Rate to be in the region of 0.23%, this paper will assume an IFR for the UK of 0.33% due to the higher rate of obesity than the global population, the UK population being more aged than the global population, and the lower levels of metabolic health found in the UK population when compared to the global population.

Further, it will be assumed that the IFR in the spring wave of the pandemic was 0.67% due to the increased impact on the care home population.

Note: while this contradicts the initial assumption that the elderly and vulnerable have been protected up to this point, the crossover will be assumed to be insignificant as those who are aged and vulnerable and who were infected in the spring wave of the pandemic are unlikely to form a significant proportion of the population as at today's date.

It will be assumed that the IFR in the winter wave of the pandemic was 0.33%, in line with the assumed UK population IFR.

It will also be assumed, as a result of the vaccine rollout, that deaths will continue to decline at a rate of 4.6% per day as has been the average decline since the peak recorded January 19th.

The total number of cases required to reach these death figures will be extrapolated for three weeks and an IFR of 0.08% will be applied to these cases due to the efficacy of the vaccine.

It will be assumed each of those deaths relates to a case that has been contracted as of today's date.

It will be assumed that those aged 0-14 form the population who had prior immunity due to the statistically insignificant number of deaths from COVID-19 arising from this population.

Finally, it will be assumed that immunity is lasting.

Modelling

Vaccinations:

1st dose: 16,423,082

2nd dose: 573,724

Immunity is calculated at $(573,724 \times 0.9) + ((16,423,082 - 573,724) \times 0.8) = 13,203,038$.

Spring cases leading to effective immunity:

Deaths up to July 31st were recorded to be 41,294. Applying an IFR of 0.67% as assumed above gives the number of suspected cases, and therefore assumed immunity, of 6,163,284.

Autumn and Winter cases leading to effective immunity

Deaths from August 1st up to February 17th were recorded as 78,091. Applying an IFR of 0.33% as assumed above gives the number of suspected cases, and therefore assumed immunity, of 23,663,939.

Future deaths leading to effective immunity

Extrapolating the deaths on the trend currently seen of a decline per day of 1.6% over the next three weeks gives a cumulative death toll of 5,736 up to March 9th. Applying the IFR of 0.08% as assumed above gives the number of suspected cases, and therefore assumed immunity of 7,170,538.

Prior immunity in the age group 0-14

The size of the population that is aged between 0-14 currently amounts to approximately 11,960,000. As stated above, this figure will be assumed to have full immunity.

Tabulation

Vaccinations	13,203,038
Spring cases	6,163,284
Autumn/Winter cases	23,663,939
Extrapolated deaths cases	7,170,538
Prior immunity	11,960,000
Total	**62,160,799**

Total population per ONS: 66,650,000

Conclusion

This model anticipates that the proportion of the population currently stands 62,160,799 / 66,650,000, or 93.3%.

There is a possibility that this figure is lower due to crossover of groups identified above.

It should also be noted that applying the WHO IFR of 0.23% throughout the pandemic results in a population immunity figure of 119.4%.

Therefore, we conclude that the population immunity figure stands at 93.3%, with a 95% confidence interval of 67.2% - 119.4%.

The Launch of *Lockdown? What Lockdown?*

22ⁿᵈ February 2021

Welcome to *Lockdown? What Lockdown?*

The Lockdown zealots, fanatics, and ZeroCovid Cult have often been spotted on social media using the phrase, "Lockdown? What Lockdown?" as they vent their misplaced fury at the individuals who have realised that their declining mental health poses a much more significant risk to their health than COVID-19 and so have decided to go for a walk in a park with a friend. We, here, on the day the roadmap out of Lockdown was announced, have decided to claim this phrase for our own.

Here at Lockdown? What Lockdown? we know all too well what the mental and societal costs of these nonsensical lockdowns have amounted to and, therefore, we want to celebrate those enterprising individuals who have done anything from found the courage to have dinner with their "bubble", or identified little loopholes in the regulations, right through to having hosted a massive party, or an illegal rave, all in the name of attempting to reclaim a sense of normality and because you, like us, believe that waiting for June 21ˢᵗ is the true definition of covidiocy.

Just as importantly as what you actually did, we also want to hear how it has helped you, made you feel better, made you more optimistic, or whatever the positive impact may have been.

On the Contact page, you will find our email address and an anonymous message box through which you can tell us anything you'd like to, entirely anonymously, from how you've bent the rules to how you've escaped the country.

We want to celebrate these stories for two reasons: the first is so that we can all share in your joyous moments; the second is to provide confidence to those still too afraid to visit friends that they can indeed find ways to enjoy life again.

Get out. See a friend. Share a hug.

I have included the first two stories posted to the website because I wrote them myself with inspiration from true stories. After the first two stories, I asked Lockdown Sceptics to share the website; they did, and I didn't need to write another story from then!

Lockdown? What Lockdown?

22nd February 2021

Our first story!

As of Thursday 18th February, I had not seen a single friend since mid-October.

To massively oversimplify, I was really struggling to cope. But then an invite came through for a dinner party. I snatched at the opportunity, not even in the slightest bit concerned with appearing "too keen", and on Friday night I found myself sat around a table with seven other people — yes, people(!) — discussing everything from the lunacy of lockdowns to the morality of vegetarianism.

I don't think it's possible to overstate how much that dinner benefitted me and my mental health, but, to give you an idea, in the space of a single evening, I went from questioning the point of continuing with life, to grinning like a fool, and laughing at the most awful jokes you will ever hear.

I can promise you now, that will not be my last dinner party of February.

Get out. See a friend. Share a hug.

Lockdown? What Lockdown?

23rd February 2021

Welcome back to day two of Lockdown? What Lockdown?

We have a real heart-warmer for you today, so I will just leave you in the capable hands of our anonymous writer.

This morning was a very special morning.

It wouldn't have been any kind of special a year ago, but a year ago, I didn't know I wouldn't see my father for the next twelve months.

For about six years, since my mother died, up until February 2020, my father would come over on Tuesday mornings for a coffee, some cake, and to simply sit and chat; and when COVID-19 hit us, he withdrew from us and stopped coming over.

Three weeks ago yesterday, though, he received his first dose of the vaccine, and has now decided that enough is enough. So, this morning, we started up our Tuesday coffee, cake, and chat mornings again.

The way it started was eerie. It felt wrong, it felt off for some reason. I think it was because we were both behaving as if we hadn't missed the last 50 or so weeks, chatting about the kids (his grandchildren), talking about plans for the future, discussing whether he would try and find a new woman.

I was halfway through a sentence when I spotted his hand was shaking as he placed his mug back on the coffee table. Naturally, I instantly started worrying — worries that weren't allayed when I looked up and saw his eyes were watering.

"Dad, what's wrong?" I asked him, the urgency apparent in my tone, I'm sure.

He looked at me and smiled.

"Nothing, my sweetness. Nothing at all. But I've made a decision. Whatever happens in the future, promise me that we won't ever give up these mornings together again. They're far too precious to me." He told me.

I did promise him as much; I promised him this as I stood up, walked around the coffee table and hugged him like a daughter should always be able to hug their father.

Get out. See a friend. Share a hug.

Why Lockdowns don't work

27th February

Many people have put forward many suggestions to the question that Chris Snowdon believes the asking of to be equivalent to "anti-science"; although, isn't the asking of questions the definition of science..?

Others have said that the onus is not on the sceptics or anti-lockdowners to provide the justification for why the lockdowns appear not to work, only to point out that the data does not support the case for lockdowns not appearing to work.

Others say that we cannot determine how much worse it would be without lockdowns; the response is to point at Sweden or Florida, at which point the doubters tell the sceptics that that isn't a fair comparison.

One argument that isn't often put forward is the very simple one of applying the IFR as set out by the WHO across 80% of the population. When 80% of a population has immunity to a virus, as is to be expected to be obtained in this case, then we achieve a robust level of the bizarrely feared "herd immunity". 0.23% applied to 80% of the UK population would leave a tragic toll of 123,000 dead.

However, given that deaths within 28 days of a positive test stand at 122,415, and deaths with COVID-19 on the death certificate stand at 135,613, it stands to reason that one can say, with a good degree of certainty, that things would not have been any worse without lockdowns.

However, we are currently in a situation where the anti-lockdowners are considered loonies by the lockdowners, and the lockdowners are considered lazy, simple, or manipulated by the mainstream media by the anti-lockdowners.

Therefore, the only way to progress is to put forward the answer to the question of why lockdowns "don't work", because otherwise, as Snowdon states in the Great Debate, we must contend with the contradiction that either it's a lack of compliance that stops the lockdowns working (and therefore we can't lay the blame for all the harms at the feet of the lockdown), or that people would have behaved as they did under lockdown with only guidelines in place instead of lockdowns.

But let's start with the issue of how people would have behaved without mandatory restrictions in place. I believe it's highly likely that had I been able to continue playing sport, seeing people in pubs, and working in the office that I would have seen fewer people at home. I also believe that had these parts of my life been left to me that I would have been able to stay in my apartment in London living alone and would not have been forced to move back home with others where the risk of the virus being brought into the home and spread there is obviously increasing with each person you live with. It's also inevitable that had I been able to continue doing my shopping online that I would have come into contact with fewer people in the supermarkets.

Can these factors be applied countrywide though? Certainly to an extent that is sufficient for them to be considered, but also certainly not to everyone in the country; what about all those who have stayed on their own in little flats in London or other major cities?

Extended periods of isolation lead to loneliness – to dispute this is to delve into anti-science. This is important not just because it is one of the many collateral damages of the lockdowns, but because loneliness is a killer. Cacioppo published a paper stating that extreme loneliness increases the risk of premature death in the elderly by 14% (three times the IFR suggested by the worst case scenarios for Covid-19 in the elderly; and Hawkley states in a 2015 paper that "Cortisol has immunosuppressive effects, and elevated cortisol levels in lonely individuals were associated with lower natural killer cell activity and poorer T-lymphocyte responses to mitogen stimulation" and that "loneliness was associated with poorer antibody response to a component of the flu vaccine."

Not only have the lockdowns increased loneliness, dramatically increasing chance of premature death, suppressing immune systems, and potentially reducing the efficacy of the vaccine, but we have been catastrophically and perpetually placed in a state of fear, further driving up cortisol levels and deepening these issues, and we have been forced to spend our time afraid indoors, away from the sun and its immunity-boosting light, and steadily gaining weight and losing fitness, adding to the nation's "underlying health conditions".

There are two other arguments I'm going to make; first is the argument around asymptomatic spread. As written up by Jonathan Engler and Clare Criag, the case for this is "woeful". The question that is therefore posed is, how much symptomatic spread have the lockdowns prevented? It stands to reason that the answer would be, not very much. If sick people are sick, then they tend not to be very keen on going out and partying with or without a lockdown.

"*But!*" Cry the lockdowners, "*we are a country notoriously bad at going to work when we have a cold!*"

Thank you, this is my final argument, and it is the same one Sir Desmond Swayne made in the commons earlier this week: when those people with mild cold symptoms don't go out and spread their softer, milder strains of the virus, those strains go out of circulation, removing the possibility of immunity that can be gained from those easily beaten strains, and leaving the population susceptible to the more aggressive strains when they have to go into hospital for any reason at all.

Now, is it necessarily the case that all I've said here is certainly, categorically and scientifically true? No, because I only have the same medical and epidemiological qualifications as Neil Ferguson, but there is more than enough in here to say with confidence that there are reasons why the lockdowns might not work, why the impact of reduced social interaction might be reversed, and without robust proof against these arguments – which does not exist, the Government does not have a legitimate claim to implement them.

So… Get out. See a friend. Share a hug.

I'm not "antivaxx", but…

3rd March 2021

I have now had three comments thrown my way in response to my stating that I have no desire to get the SARS-CoV-2 jab: one just outright accusing me of being "antivaxx"; one which went something like, "see, now you're stepping into antivaxx territory"; and one which went something like, "so, I assume you're antivaxx, then?"

The problem with discussing anything with these kinds of people is that they make their assumptions early, and then one is forced to battle their preconceived notions, rather than inform, educate, and persuade on anything resembling a level-playing field for debate.

It is the same with discussing lockdowns from a position of being anti-lockdown; first you have to convince your esteemed interlocuter that you are not insane before they will pay any attention to your "ideas and opinions". Pointing out that I am not putting forward "ideas and opinions", but rather conclusions that it seems inconceivable anyone would be able to disagree with were they to investigate for themselves and have access to all the same information appears to carry no weight either.

And so, it seems, every debate regarding the vaccine has to start with the phrase, "I'm not antivaxx, but…"

I thought I would outline my "buts" here.

First up is one that I never thought would need to be specified, but, unfortunately, appears is necessary: not wanting one vaccine does not an antivaxxer make.

As a gay man, I am more susceptible to the HPV virus; however, there is only one place in the country a man can get the HPV vaccine (or, at least, there was when I decided to get it): the MSM clinic in Brighton. It is also a three-shot vaccine and each trip down took a total of four hours, but I was happy to give up twelve hours of my life to significantly reduce my risk of contracting this nasty virus.

This neatly leads onto my second point. Every medical procedure an individual goes through should be based on a personal risk assessment. In the case of the SARS-CoV-2 virus, having already contracted it and recovered in a matter of days, I see my risk of not having the vaccine as being as close to nil as is scientifically possible. Based on everything I am seeing regarding the vaccine, on balance, I see my risk of taking the vaccine as tiny; most likely, I have a sore arm and possibly a bit of a headache for a day or two. However, a tiny risk is still greater than an infinitesimal one; and so, based on my personal risk assessment, not getting the vaccine wins out against getting the vaccine.

This leads into my third argument, which is more principled: I will not get any medical procedure on the basis that "my" Government wants me to have it.

Indeed, the very fact that the Government is attempting to coerce individuals into abandoning their right to make their own personal risk assessments regarding a medical intervention encourages me to stand against this on principle, effectively abandoning my own personal risk assessment and simply saying "no". This is anti-big-state, not antivaxx.

In the raging hypothetical where the data were clear, where the risk of the vaccine was minimal, where the virus posed a greater risk to my age group (under 30s) than it does, and where the risk of re-infection was greater than it appears to be, but where the Government was still attempting to coerce individuals into taking the vaccine, then I would still be opposed to taking it.

The final argument I have is more forward looking, and less personal. While it appears to still be up for debate what the Government is attempting to do regarding the Lockdowns, if one were to extrapolate from my essay Opportunity, Incentive, and Rationalisation, then a reasonable conclusion to draw would be that they are seeking a way of ensuring that the only explanation for escaping this "pandemic" is the vaccines that they so expertly sourced, secured, and rolled out in a bid to vindicate their actions over the last twelve months.

If this is the case, then the greater the number of individuals who refuse the vaccine, the harder claiming that narrative becomes, and the harder it is for the Government to claim this narrative, the less likely it is that they will be able to escape justice for all the harms they've caused over the last twelve months.

I am not antivaxx, but I am pro-debate, I am pro-individual choice based on risk assessments regarding medical procedures, I am anti-big-state, I am anti-fraud, and I am pro-justice, and it is on these grounds that I will refuse the SARS-CoV-2 vaccine.

The weekend of 5th March 2021

Here follows a debate published in Lockdown?
What Lockdown?

For (opening statement): I will confess that I wore a mask up until October, despite my awareness of the evidence highlighting the futility of the act. I will also confess to the panic I felt when first I walked into a petrol station face-naked: the fear of censure, reprimand, or confrontation increasing my heart rate and blood pressure to what was surely an unhealthy level.

By the latter confession, it would appear that, under the mask mandate exemption specification of "severe distress" – as pointed out in our previous story, I would more likely qualify for an exemption from walking into a shop maskless than for not wearing a mask. However, there is a very reasonable argument to be made that I do qualify for exemption under the specification of "severe distress": this entire situation has caused me severe distress, and the idea of conforming with the mask mandate, by extension, also causes me severe distress.

But, whether I'm legally exempt from participating in an almost cultish, ritualistic, and anti-scientific Government mandate or not is secondary to this debate. The question is whether we who do refuse to participate should make the very easy purchase of an exemption lanyard and wear that lanyard as and when the mask mandate applies.

I believe not, and I will make three points to support this belief.

The first is that there are those who are legitimately exempt because of PTSD, claustrophobia, anxiety, and other conditions, as well as those who spend time with the deaf and hard of hearing who rely on lip reading. There is something unsettling about pretending to be one among these individuals, and I believe doing so undermines the legitimacy of the claims to exemption of those who would be greatly negatively impacted were they forced into compliance. We are not exempt because of the masks themselves causing severe distress, but because the compliance itself causes severe distress, and a statement of this fact can be made by not wearing a lanyard.

The second point follows on from this, because there is value in this statement of non-compliance. In wearing a lanyard, the wearer is showing the Government that they are happy to play their game; but I put to you the point that we shouldn't be playing their game at all. I will play Tesco's game, and tell any security guard who asks if I have a mask that I am exempt, but this is different, and also a very rare occurrence. By not wearing a lanyard though, you are stating your refusal to engage in the Government's nonsense at any level, and when every part of the mask mandate is nonsense, not participating in any way at all is the optimal course of action.

My third point concerns others with whom one might come into contact with, fleetingly or otherwise. If our ultimate goal, regarding this debate, is to put an end to the mask mandate, the quickest route is for the majority to simply stop wearing them. By wearing a lanyard, there is a risk of signalling a held belief that only those who are legitimately exempt should be the only ones not wearing masks. By not wearing a lanyard, on the other hand, it is an invitation to all other shoppers who agree that they're pointless to rip them off and push the fight for normality one step closer in the right direction.

In conclusion, I am for the proposed motion because in refusing to wear a lanyard a distinction is made between you and those suffering from mental health issues, a statement of non-compliance and refusal to participate in cultish behaviour is made, and the route out of the mask mandate is expedited.

Against (opening statement): Thank you Mr Editor.

We can, and do, agree that wearing masks is degrading, dehumanising, at best irritating (and at worst genuinely distressing, if not, for most of us, "severely" so), and, according to all available evidence, essentially pointless. So it is both reasonable and rational for a person not to wear a mask. I acknowledge that I am very happy not to wear a mask but will wear a lanyard in certain places.

Whether a person, having decided not to wear a mask "should" or "should not" then wear, or not wear, a lanyard is open to an analysis on (at least) two different levels. The first is the ideological argument in your first two points. The second is the practical argument in your third point.

As regards your first point, you may be unsettled, but I struggle to see why it is objectively unsettling. I am not unsettled, for example. Nor do I see how it undermines the legitimacy of the exemption claimed by the genuinely exempt. Surely there are genuinely exempt out there who do not wear lanyards? And I am less distressed by the compliance than I am by the bloody mask – and I suspect I am not alone.

As regards your second point, I agree that it is all nonsense, and support you making your statement to the world. Will it listen? I fear not.

Your third point is where we both converge and diverge. I take it that our ultimate goal is not simply to end this silly mask mandate, but to show to people that they can live their lives untrammelled by petty, pointless restrictions.

So how best to do that? I believe that many wear masks because (1) they do not wish to discomfort others and (2) they are archetypically British and feel uncomfortable breaking rules. Wearing a lanyard, I think, negates (1). Much more importantly, it allows them to start breaking rules in a small way (as they are essentially telling an untruth), which will enable them to move on to greater breaches. It is a gateway drug.

(And when Wendy at the garage asked me to wear a lanyard because otherwise her boss would have a go at her, I did so, because it really isn't her fault.)

For (rebuttal and closing statement): Thank you for your opening statement. I believe there are a number of points worth raising as regards your rebuttal to my first ideological point – as you put it.

The first is that I agree that it cannot be objectively unsettling; this is an emotional reaction, and therefore can only be subjective.

Further, I will concede that, as there will surely be those who are legitimately exempt and choose not to wear a lanyard, wearing a lanyard while not legitimately being exempt cannot entirely undermine the legitimacy of others' exemptions. However, it does undermine the statement that I wish to make.

Which brings us to your second point that while supporting my statement, you cynically fear the world will take no notice.

I don't naively expect every person I pass by face-naked and sans-lanyard to see me and instinctively assume that I am protesting the Government's actions and the mask mandate; however, I do expect people to notice. A maskless individual, after all, stands out from the crowd these days. My view is that a maskless individual wearing a lanyard stands out less, and so, if by not wearing a lanyard I can make a slightly bigger drop in the ocean, then that size differential is worthwhile.

As regards your point that wearing a lanyard negates the discomfort felt by others upon seeing a maskless individual, I remain unconvinced. Too many of those who would be discomfited will assume the lanyard is a lie and the wearer simply a fool taking the Michie.

The comments on social media exclaiming that mask-exempt individuals should not be allowed in the shops at all attest to this belief.

As regards your penultimate point that there are many current mask wearers who are aware of the pointlessness but feel uncomfortable breaking the rules, and that the lanyard can act as a "gateway drug" to greater breaches that will see the toppling of all petty, pointless restrictions, I see the merit in this argument; however, I believe it to be flawed on two levels.

The first is that, given the ridicule the lanyard has received, many will not perceive it to have the protective qualities and to be a sufficient excuse for the wearer that your argument attributes to it; and the second is that while it may be telling an untruth, it is still telling that untruth within the parameters of the petty, pointless restrictions, and, because of this, it seems less like a "gateway" through which one can pass onto greener pastures, and more like a window that can be cracked open while still remaining indoors, abiding by the stay at home order.

Ultimately, the point I am making is this: I do not believe the merits of the lanyard are either as present or as great as you seem to believe they are. I do believe, however, that removing the mask, not wearing a lanyard, and tasting that liberation in its purity can act as a "gateway drug" to the greater breaches you mention.

As regards your final and uncharacteristically personal point; no, it is not Wendy's fault that we are living under a despotic regime that has convinced its public through a campaign of fear that it is right for individuals to be coerced into wearing notifications of medical conditions for all to see – whether legitimate or an "untruth"; but in capitulating to Wendy's boss' demands, this aspect of the current dystopia is only perpetuated. Meaningful change for the better has never been brought about by appeasement.

I will conclude by saying this: a lanyard may ease the way to living lives untrammelled by petty, pointless restrictions; not wearing a lanyard may not make a screeching statement to all observers; but we are past the point of "easy does it", it is time to rip the plaster clean off; and, in doing so, and in making at least some small statement, at least some little good may come of it.

Against (rebuttal and closing statement): Before closing, I would make a few observations:

1.   a cynic is what an idealist calls a realist;

2.   I am not persuaded that comments on social media are representative of the population as a whole, or should be taken into account in any analysis;

3.   we are both aware (having had the same primary source) that the "ridicule the lanyard has received" is from a person who would not be prepared to go maskless in public in any circumstances. That ridicule rings a little hollow.

Having said all that, I think only two issues remain:

First, how are people to be persuaded that they can safely and reasonably ignore the rules and regain their lives? Starting with giant strides in admirable, but baby steps are easier. I find it easier to go maskless in some situations with a lanyard than without. The situations in which I am prepared to go completely mask and lanyard free are increasing. It is baby steps; I can do those.

Secondly, and the only real reason why I do find that approach easier, is that I wasn't capitulating to Wendy's boss's demands – I was being solicitous of Wendy. Maybe collateral damage is sometimes necessary, but I would rather not be the person inflicting it.

So I think the question for our readers is this – which route is more likely to end with a mask (and lanyard) free society that openly treats other rules with the respect they deserve – the shock and awe approach of the Covid Liberation Front, trampling over poor Wendy's job prospects, or the hearts and minds approach of the lanyard-wearers, with Gandhi, Mandela, and Martin Luther-King as their role models?

We Must Strive For The Return of Trust

6th March 2021

Published in Lockdown Sceptics 8th March 2021

This essay aims to highlight and address a single issue, and so, for that purpose, let us assume that the Government's response to the SARS-CoV-2 virus has not set a precedent of how to deal with pandemics that sees the same response occurring every five to ten years when new viruses emerge with similar pathogen profiles; let us assume that our economy bounces back in a drastic way; let us assume that our personal health data isn't tracked in a truly unnecessary way; and let us assume everything else that would need to be assumed in order for our old normal to be returned to us unfettered.

Further, let us assume that the roadmap out of this ludicrous insanity can be trusted, that our Prime Minister can be trusted when he says that this is the last Lockdown, and that when we get to June 21st, if not before, we really are entirely done with every tangible aspect of this for good.

Even with these SAGE-level assumptions, we are left with one very significant issue that will keep us distinctly separated from the old normal: trust – in all its guises; and that is what I plan to discuss here.

We shall meander down two hypothetical paths in this essay: the first looks at the possibility that there is no public inquiry, or that any public inquiry vindicates the Government's actions; and the second looks at the possibility that there is a public inquiry and it finds the lockdowns to have been a catastrophic mistake.

Under the first hypothetical, very few of us on the anti-lockdown side of the debate will find it possible to trust the results of the public inquiry, but more than this, very few will find it possible to trust Government in the same way again.

I drove up to Uxbridge from Surrey yesterday, and as I whipped around the M25, where there would normally have been about fifty road signs ordering me to STAY HOME SAVE LIVES, there were only two. My reading of this was not that the messaging had been removed by mistake, or anything else so innocent, but, instead, that this massive reduction was part of yet another Government psy-op, subtly gearing up to prepare people for the removal of the stay-at-home order. This cynicism can only be described as a symptom of the lack of trust I have for this Government.

I was slow to question the Lockdown in the beginning in the most part because I was slow to question my Government, its competence and its motives, and just like in any relationship, losing trust is much easier than regaining it.

Further, we must consider what this hypothetical situation will mean for the trust between fellow citizens. Many of us on the anti-lockdown side of the debate will have lost friends over this; if we are not vindicated publicly, will it be possible to regain those friendships? If not, what use is it having the pubs back open to us if we cannot share in the revelry with all those we used to?

Third, we must consider the fear, or the people's trust in safety. It has been well documented that the fear levels in the UK have surpassed any other country, and the pressing question therefore, is how quickly will our offices, restaurants, naked faces, pubs and clubs rebound upon the Government announcement that they can indeed return "safely"?

There is a strong argument to be made that those who believed the Government up until now, and therefore form the most fearful portion of the population, will believe the Government when told there is no longer any need to be fearful; however, there is also a strong possibility that clubs or stadia will take years to return to sell-out capacity as people continue to perceive fellow healthy humans as little more than vectors for disease.

Under the second hypothetical where the lockdowns are ruled to have been a mistake, these issues remain; however, the lack of trust in Government will be much more pervasive – so much so, that trust in democracy itself may be rocked; it will be we who need to forgive our counterparts who sat on the then found to be wrong side of the fence; and there is a risk that those who were most fearful will struggle to accept the message that there no longer exists a justified reason to be so afraid.

A recent post in Lockdown Sceptics discussed the risk that trust in doctors to have their patients' best interests at heart will be diminished, but the issues run deeper: what about trust in law and order when it will have been shown that the laws set out by the Government were unfounded and nonsensical? What about trust in the news, or the mainstream media, when they will have been shown to have been somewhere on the spectrum between complicit and negligent? What about trust in freedom of speech, the foundation of democracy, when the risk of censorship, censure, or being cancelled has run so high throughout the past twelve months?

Two significant risks to trust remain irrespective of which hypothetical path we find ourselves on in the future. The first is our trust in ourselves for those who have developed mental health issues during this time. For many, a return to normality will see the eradication of depressive symptoms, heightened cortisol, stress, and anxiety; however, for many others, these issues will persist. A year ago, I was discussing with others how I believed my depression to be healed, and how I expected that I would never again experience a depressive episode. Now, I am unsure I have the capacity or the trust in myself to live alone again, and, ironically, I will not be alone in this.

The second significant risk to trust is generational. School closures and the vilification of students, among many other examples, have unforgivably – in the eyes of many – placed the safety of older generations over the needs of our young. This neglect, quite understandably so, is unlikely to be forgotten in a flash.

If we are to truly reclaim our Old Normal, then the reestablishment of trust must lie at the very heart of that reclamation, and there is no simple and easy fix.

As we move forward, we must once again put our children first, we must strive to forgive and support our fellow citizen, we must fight for our freedom of speech, encouraging alternative viewpoints and debate, and we must push for greater engagement in politics that brings about true transparency and a return of true democracy where those who govern do so on behalf of, and within the interests of the governed. Only with each of these efforts can normality truly return.

Given an inch, I'm going to take a mile

10th March 2021

The Government's roadmap may be moving at a glacial pace, especially as Scotland starts to accelerate its unlocking; however, there are a few gems hidden within it – loopholes, if you will – if you look closely and creatively enough.

Step 1a – 8 March

From 8 March, schools returned, and we were permitted to leave home for a picnic with one other individual not in our household or support bubble. We all know about these; however, also added to the easing of restrictions was that *"Wraparound childcare and other supervised children's activities can resume where they enable parents to work, seek work, attend education, seek medical care or attend a support group."*

This means that you would be well within your legal rights were you to organise an activity for your child and your friends' children that would allow you to discuss, in person and with those friends, a certain business idea you might be keen on pursuing with said friends. If that should take the shape of a playdate for the kids and a dinner party for the adults, well, so be it – it's not as if you can host a business meeting in a restaurant right now.

The additional easing that comes on 29 March includes outdoor sports (where formally organised) to resume, and the rule of six (or two households) to return, including for private gardens.

This is the date that the Stay-at-Home order will be lifted, and, also, I believe the date the nation will reach critical mass on non-compliance as enforcement of the rules on private gatherings will become too difficult; however, we are looking at legal loopholes here, not outright non-compliance.

So, here's what I'm thinking… The five individuals who you have over for a BBQ on 29 March will, of course, be permitted entry to the home in order to pass through to the garden. Once you've kindly permitted your guests entry to your home, I suggest you ensure they get lost on the way to the garden, ideally somewhere around the dining table, or the living room; while getting lost in a strange place is always stressful, were they to spend the entire day "passing through the home on the way to the garden", that would appear to be within the rules come 29 March.

Step 2 – 12 April

The current plan will see a fair few restrictions lifted in Step 2 on 12 April, including pub gardens, gyms, zoos, theme parks, non-essential retail, hairdressers and so on, and so the need for loopholes starts to dwindle.

However, there is one restriction easing that I plan to take advantage of: "Funerals can continue with up to 30 people, and the numbers able to attend weddings, receptions, and commemorative events such as wakes will rise to 15 (from 6)."

While funerals must, it seems, take place at a registered address, at no point is it specified where such commemorative events must take place, and so, from 12 April, I plan to hold weekly wakes for the passing of my great friends Civil Liberties, Common Sense, and Inalienable Rights. Their passing has caused me immeasurable grief, and I fear I will need to mourn this loss on a regular basis – until such a day arrives that they may be revived.

Step 3 – 17 May

Come 17 May, as per the Government's roadmap, my life will be largely, and practically, unaffected; however, my weekly wakes can be extended to thirty people by this point.

Step 4 – 21 June

I won't speculate this far, not least because the language in the roadmap changes and becomes somewhat worrisome as each easing of restrictions includes the words "we hope to", as opposed to steps 1-3 which uses the words "it will be"; you will forgive me for not having too much faith in this Government's "hopes" at this point.

Risk of mortality in patients infected with SARS-CoV-2 variant of concern 202012/1: matched cohort study

10ᵗʰ March 2021

Here follows an email chain between me and one of the authors of the paper published in the BMJ named as above

R,

I am concerned about a number of elements in your recently published paper in the BMJ and I would be very grateful if you could clarify these for me.

Starting with the participants pairing: was any consideration given to underlying health conditions? The paper states that pairing was done on the basis of age, sex, ethnicity, deprivation, region, and sample date; but when >90% of all COVID-19 deaths have had at least one comorbidity, surely this would be a crucial factor for consideration?

Further, what consideration was given to infectiousness? Of the 54,906 matched pairs of participants, were the positive specimens confirmed with a second test, and were the cycle thresholds recorded? An individual testing positive at a CT value of 30 surely could not have been matched with an individual testing positive at a CT value of 20? The paper states that sampling was restricted to only tests that reported a cycle threshold value of <30, so, this was possible, was it not? Admittedly, as those who were S gene negative had a lower mean CT value, the number of matched pairs would have had to have been reduced to accommodate this.

Moving onto the results section. The sample population were all over thirty; so it seems misleading to not state this in the results and suggest that the results are representative of the wider community.

I can see that the 141 S gene positive deaths has to increase by 61% to reach the 227 S positive deaths, can you confirm why (141 / 54906)*1000 was rounded down from 2.568 to 2.5? This is how the 64% figure is obtained, but it seems like there is a fairly significant rounding error in there.

Next, can you explain to me where the imaginary individual came from? I am referring to how, within the S gene negative population of 54,906 individuals, 54,680 survived and 227 died. This is 54,907… so, I ask again, where has this extra person come from? Did someone die twice?

I am also concerned about the misleading representation of these results. Should we present this as survivability reduced in the B.1.1.7 variant, then we would see that this is a 0.155% reduction in survivability — and I assure you, there is no rounding error in that calculation.

Finally on the results section, and this is just my sceptical mind flagging up a potentially curious coincidence. What was the split in sex of the S gene positive and S gene negative deaths? I just noticed that 141 women died and 227 men died; while 141 S positive individuals died and 227 S negative individuals died. That seemed odd to me.

Just to briefly touch on the conclusions...

You make the following sweeping statement: "infection with VOC-202012/1 has the potential to cause substantial additional mortality compared with previously circulating variants." I fear that this statement neglects to take into consideration either our progress with the vaccine rollout or our progress towards herd immunity through prior infection. We have been assured that the vaccine is effective against the B.1.1.7 variant, therefore, we can assume prior infection from previous strains will equally provide immunity to this variant.

You also make this statement: "Healthcare capacity planning and national and international control policies are all impacted by this finding, with increased mortality lending weight to the argument that further coordinated and stringent measures are justified to reduce deaths from SARS-CoV-2." Yes, I am sure that this paper will impact Government policy, and not for the better. There is plenty of evidence that the more stringent measures have very little, if any, impact on COVID mortality — see this summary from the AIER should you feel so inclined. Therefore, irrespective of the findings of this paper, more stringent measures are never justified.

Kind regards,

Jonny

Thanks for the feedback

There is a rounding error in the numbers in the table. Although it reports exact numbers because we used 50 different combinations of pairs the figures presented are actually an average. We didn't think it necessary to present the decimal places but agree it adds confusion, and will seek to clarify.

I have investigated the 141 / 227 M/F and S-/+ issue and have to conclude it is coincidence. I'm still looking into it though.

We did not have data on comorbidities (it is mentioned in the limitations) There is another paper in the pipeline which did look at them and found no additional effect.

Dr R

Dr R,

Apologies for missing your title on the previous email.

You are very welcome for the feedback — it made for an entertaining evening reviewing your paper that calls for more stringent measures, seeing as how I have very little else to do because of the very stringent measures already in place; so, thank you for that; and thank you for your reply.

I would always include decimal places — it stops us pedants getting all excited over things that turn out to be nothing.

Thank you for clarifying these points as well, particularly the comorbities point that I missed clarification of in the paper itself. I look forward to reading this paper that's in the pipeline when it does come out. However, I do feel I should ask regarding the M/F and S-/+ coincidence, how can you have both concluded on a matter and still be looking into it?

Can I just quickly follow up on the points not addressed in your reply? Those being pair matching on CT values, the misleading nature of the cohort sample age vs population age, the misleading nature of reporting on mortality rates instead of survivability rates, immunity levels in the community, and more stringent measures being implemented.

Given the fact that this paper will likely be quoted in one of those press conferences soon, I do feel these are important points that should be addressed.

Kind regards,

Jonny

I received no further response.

What might I have got wrong?

12th March 2021

Over recent weeks, I have sought out debate because I want the fundamental tenets of what I'm confident about to be challenged – constantly, and it appears that those who would stand against my views are quick to flee from debate. Perhaps they believe I am so deluded that it is not worth stooping to my level; perhaps they are unwilling to fully engage with the debate; or perhaps they lack the wit to fully engage.

Regardless of their reasons for not challenging my views, it is the duty of anyone of a scientific mind to question, because to cease to question is to cease to learn.

Therefore, I will often ask of myself the most challenging questions as regards my position on lockdowns to really assess my views.

In the interest of time though, I will only focus on one major aspect in this piece: the efficacy of lockdowns. It is my position that the lockdowns have been ineffective at reducing Covid morbidity, hospitalisations, and transmission. This is based on the 30+ studies compiled by the AIER, the fact that the disease is fast becoming primarily nosocomial, the fact that isolation drives up loneliness which has a catastrophic impact on people's immune systems, and the fact that each of the lockdowns were imposed after the best estimates of symptomatic infection peaks. See the below graph from the REACT-2 Round 5 paper with the dates of lockdowns superimposed:

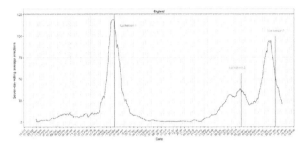

Dr Clare Craig pointed out recently that it's possible to push those lockdown imposition lines out by five days further as this is the average number of days between transmission and onset of symptoms; although, you will note, this isn't even necessary to illustrate the point.

However, if I were to challenge myself in a way that doesn't involve the usual "argument" of, "lockdowns work because of course they work", then I would point out that none of the lockdowns were implemented without prior seeding. On the 9th March, Italy entered its first national lockdown and soon after this date our media started baying for Boris Johnson to do the same; on the 16th March, the Government told people to "stop non-essential contact and travel"; and on the 19th March, Boris Johnson said that the UK could turn the tide on coronavirus in 12 weeks (the plan was never a three-week lockdown).

The REACT-2 graph above shows symptomatic infections first peaking on the 20th March.

Is it possible that sufficient numbers of people were sufficiently anxious that they began acting as if we were in lockdown between the dates of Italy's lockdown on the 9th March and the Government's "stop non-essential contact and travel" message on the 16th March for that to have been the driving factor in bringing infections down?

This line of questioning can be applied to peaks 2 and 3 with the graph showing symptomatic infections peaking for the second and third times respectively on the 3rd November and 29th December. Although Lockdown 2 wasn't imposed until November 5th, it was announced on October 31st, and although Lockdown 3 wasn't imposed until January 6th, we all knew it was imminent by the time Christmas was cancelled.

This, I believe, is the strongest argument against my case possessed by those who support the lockdowns. One cannot even employ the intuitive riposte to this, being, of course, to say that this is evidence that guidance instead of rules would have been sufficient, because the psychological tactics employed by the Government were so effective that, realistically, the lockdowns were de facto imposed the moment they were seeded, and these tactics could never have been so effective a second and third time had the

Government not followed through with the first Lockdown.

Further, it could be argued that I have fallen foul of contradictory logic by claiming that Covid-19 fast becoming a primarily nosocomial disease is a reason why lockdowns would be ineffective, as the counter-argument could be that the only reason it is indeed becoming primarily nosocomial is because lockdowns in the community have been effective, while hospitals, of course, have had to remain open, and that, therefore, had wider communities remained open too, we would see hospital transmission being representative of the wider community.

However, as this argument relies on the assumed efficacy of lockdowns, the answer to this question will come out upon the conclusion regarding the seeding argument, so I will revert my attention to that.

As regards this challenge – the one I believe to be the strongest against my case, it appears to fall apart quickly once you take into consideration the mobility data which has varied significantly in its drop below the baseline across the three lockdowns, while also not appearing to be particularly synchronised with the seeding dates. And, even if there was consistency in timing and variation across the lockdowns, the latest paper added to the AIER list shows no statistically significant correlation between mobility data declines and Covid mortality.

Further, the biggest flaw in this challenge is that it makes the common fallacy of being too narrow-sighted and not considering other countries in the wider international picture, because however effective the Government's psychological tactics were, they could not possibly have worked overseas.

We have seen, many times now, the graph that shows that the UK lockdown was "so effective that it simultaneously worked in Sweden too", but take a look at the graph below for what happens when you superimpose the new "cases" per million 7-day rolling average curves for the UK (full lockdown), Florida (fully open), and Nevada (halfway house).

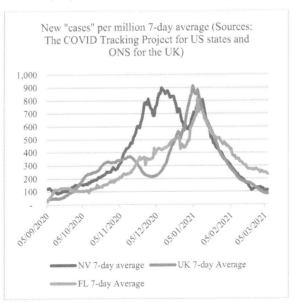

New "cases" per million 7-day average (Sources: The COVID Tracking Project for US states and ONS for the UK)

The cases per million in the UK are practically indistinguishable from those in Nevada from mid-January to now, despite Nevada starting its reopening on February 15th, with 35% capacity being permitted for indoor dining, gyms, and similar establishments, 50% capacity permitted for places of worship, galleries, medicinal and recreational cannabis establishments etc., and no limits of outdoor dining.

Admittedly, the cases per million in Florida do not appear to be falling as quickly as the UK and Nevada; however, this is most likely tied to their slower incline in cases, not to their openness. It requires some impressive mental gymnastics to claim that cases must be coming down slower because they're open without believing that being open would therefore lead to faster increases in cases – which did not happen.

Further, if we were to employ our own narrow-sighted myopia, given that the rate of decline in the UK and Nevada is practically identical, the argument could be made that the UK could be opening on the same timeline as Nevada without impacting our case data in the slightest.

But most important for this debate is the timing: all three coincide in early January; and more countries or states can be added here with South Africa peaking January 11th, Sweden peaking January 8th, Arizona and California peaking days after Nevada just to name a few. The reason this is so important is because it strongly suggests that the seeding and psychological tactics employed by the Government in the UK could not have been a sufficiently impactful strategy, and therefore, taking this in conjunction with the mobility data variances, it is not possible to bring the Lockdown imposition lines forward in the first graph as the seeding theory requires to make a case in favour of the lockdowns' efficacy.

In turn, this means that each lockdown was imposed post-peak and could not have had any impact in "turning the tide", or curbing growth of cases. Not only this, but no observable deviation in the downward curve (other than a small and bizarre uptick in cases a few days after each lockdown's imposition) suggests that the lockdowns did little to nothing to accelerate the decline or maintain the decline; or, in other words, they were ineffective, had no part to play in the disease becoming primarily nosocomial, were imposed too early (as in, by being imposed at all), not too late as Boris has been saying lately, and they did nothing to "protect the NHS from being overwhelmed".

I will, of course, continue to question and challenge my views on the lockdowns; however, for now, it appears I am secure in sticking to my guns.

Some basic maths on the testing

14th March 2021

A very simple concept that isn't often talked about, perhaps because it's intuitive, is that at any given point, the minimum number of positive results produced by the mass testing programme will be when every single one is a false positive.

This can be highlighted as follows:

If x = true positives; y = false positives; C = total "cases" reported; and T = total tests performed, then y is always a function of the false positive rate, T and x, being the false positive rate multiplied by total tests less true positives.

True positives + false positives = total "cases":

$$x + y = C$$

Can therefore be rewritten as:

$$x + (FPR * (T - x)) = C$$

Which can be rewritten as:

$$(1 - FPR)x + (FPR * T) = C$$

As the False Positive Rate can never be higher than 100% (or '1' in the function above), this shows us that whenever x (true cases) grows, so too must total cases, thus proving that total cases will be at its lowest when the 'true cases' figure is equal to zero.

This is important to note because it allows us to perform some basic modelling on the tests currently being performed.

Taking the 11th March as an example, from the Government website, we can see the following breakdown of tests performed:

Pillar 1 (NHS and, in England, PHE): 85,550

Pillar 2 (UK Government testing programme): 1,511,972

Pillar 3 (Antibody): 2,490

Pillar 4 (Surveillance): 18,347

For simplicity, we will only look at the 1,511,972 tests performed as part of Pillar 2, as the false positive rate will likely vary across the four pillars.

Also from the Government website, we can see that 334,345 PCR tests were conducted on the 11th March and that these tests were performed across pillars 1, 2, and 4. We will therefore assume that the PCR tests performed in pillar 2 number 230,448 (being the 334,345 less the 85,550 in pillar 1 and the 18,347 is pillar 4).

This suggests that the remaining 1,281,524 tests performed in pillar 2 were Lateral Flow Tests.

Applying the concept from the start of this paper, where the lowest number of total cases reported will be when the 'true cases' figure is equal to zero, and applying the low-end FPRs for PCR and LFT of 0.8% and 0.32% respectively, we see the following:

PCR tests: 0.8% * 230,448 = 1,843

Lateral Flow tests: 0.32% * 1,281,524 = 4,101

Total = 5,944

Per the Government website, the total number of "Cases by specimen date" reported on the 11th March was 5,197, or to be clear, 747 cases fewer than would be expected by applying the low-end false positive rates of the PCR and Lateral Flow tests to obtain the minimum expected figure of total cases reported.

There are four caveats to this statement, however: the first is that the 11th March falls in the "highlighted in grey" area, meaning that the figures will be updated; the second is that individuals who tested positive more than once are only counted once in the "cases by specimen date" reported figures; the third is that the Government website does not split the "cases by specimen date" into the four pillars; and the fourth, of course, is that we have not taken 106,387 tests from pillars 1, 3, and 4 into account.

It should also be noted that this modelling takes no notice of false negatives, or of the accuracy of LFTs, which, when administered by untrained individuals at home appear to have an accuracy of roughly 50%. This would, of course, reduce the false positives figure in LFTs significantly, and allow for some true positives to enter the figures in the conclusion.

That being said, from the modelling performed here, it is difficult to make any conclusion other than x, true positives, must be extremely small and tending towards zero now.

Have the Lockdowns worked in any way?

16th March 2021

This will be my final essay for this book, and I plan to look at the three major metrics by which the Lockdowns can be assessed to try and conclude whether there is any way in which the Lockdowns have achieved anything of merit.

Let's start with total COVID-19 mortality.

Using data from Our World in Data, and only looking at the most heavily impacted 50 countries, the UK falls 5th:

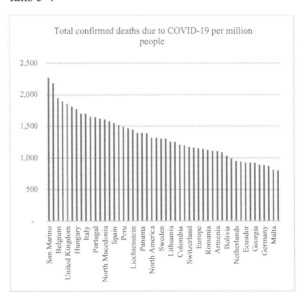

Total confirmed deaths due to COVID-19 per million people

The picture is obviously bleaker when we consider all countries, and it becomes very difficult to draw any merit of the Lockdowns using this metric.

However, if we move on to our second metric and consider all-cause excess mortality, we see a slightly different picture.

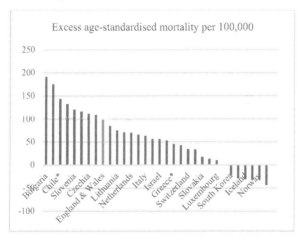

Using data from the Centre for Evidence-Based Medicine and ordering countries by excess age-standardised mortality per 100,000, England and Wales combined appears to be a little more average. However, having still performed worse than so many other countries, we should not take solace simply in the fact that more countries appear to have performed worse than us using this metric over the confirmed COVID-19 deaths metric.

Knowing that there is no meaningful correlation between stringency of measures and COVID-19 mortality tells us, in theory, that we would have performed no worse, in terms of mortality, had we not locked down, but these graphs really hammer that message home as there is very little scope to have actually performed worse.

Asking if we could have performed better is important, however, there are of course few graphs that I can use.

We can theorise though because Neil Ferguson's model predicting 510,000 lives to be lost to this virus was based on two incredibly dodgy assumptions: that prior immunity stood at 0%, and that the Infection Fatality Rate of the virus was as high as 3%.

It seems peculiar that the lead scientists can stand up on the BBC and deny the existence of prior immunity from, say, the four endemic coronaviruses that return each winter, but then tell the country that the AstraZeneca vaccine that is made of cold chimpanzee adenovirus is capable of priming the injectee with T-cells capable of fighting the SARS-CoV-2 virus.

Certain studies have suggested that prior immunity could have been as high as 50%, however, we will use a reasonable 25% for prudence. This 25% includes the younger generations (under 14s) who have been shown to not be at any risk.

Considering that a robust level of herd immunity is achieved at 80% of a population being immune, we would therefore expect that once 55% of the population (roughly 37,000,000) had been infected and could be added to the 25% assumed to have prior immunity, herd immunity would be achieved.

Applying a much more sensible IFR of 0.3% to these unfortunate 37,000,000 results in a theoretical 111,000 tragic deaths.

So, the question remains, have we saved *any* lives?

It would appear not.

That said, the original aim of the first Lockdown was to "flatten the curve" and "protect the NHS", spreading out the COVID mortality without necessarily reducing it and although the NHS was clearly stressed, at no point was it overwhelmed; so, perhaps, by this metric, the Lockdowns will appear less pointless.

Alas, they don't. We have multiple studies suggesting that the Lockdowns have not impacted on SARS-CoV-2 transmission, while also having multiple approaches that suggest each Lockdown was introduced post-infections peak.

If the Lockdowns were introduced after an infections peak, then they certainly could not retrospectively flatten that peak, and if infections had peaked prior to Lockdowns being introduced and the NHS was not overwhelmed at any point, then the Lockdowns cannot be credited in any meaningful way with having protected the NHS.

It could be argued, however, that in locking down, and reducing the number of people visiting hospitals for reasons other than COVID-19, we have reduced the burden on the NHS, potentially also reducing nosocomial infections; however, with two thirds of all hospitalised cases thought to have been caught in hospitals anyway, and a waiting list for treatment now surpassing 400,000, this is a tough circle to square.

In short, there are no gains.

This being the case, there is little need to analyse the costs, because any cost would exceed the gains of zero; however, it is still worth remembering the costs, even if for no other reason than to pay tribute to all those who have been so catastrophically impacted.

Before I do take a short look at the costs other than the massive NHS waiting list that will sadly include so many that will never be seen, it should be noted that, as we are only one year on from the first Lockdown it would be impossible to have a full grasp on every cost; there will be many that I miss here, and many more that no one would be able to predict.

But let us try regardless.

The waiting list is representative of those who have missed out on treatments, and there is an unconfirmed death toll already suffered associated with this that is estimated at 42,000. This is the number of avoidable deaths caused by denying healthcare to the population for the majority of the last twelve months, and this number can only grow as those on the waiting list find themselves never "getting their turn".

A recent coalition of cancer charities has estimated that there are 45,000 people living with cancer in the UK who are unaware of their condition and who should have started treatment last year.

There is an unconfirmed suicide toll that will be horrifying when the final figures for 2020 are released around September this year, and it should be noted that suicide is not the only cost of mental illness; a year with depression is barely worth half of a year without.

And depression is hardly the only mental health cost of the Lockdowns. The links between social media and mental health disorders are clearly drawn, and the past year has seen a much greater reliance on virtual interaction.

Not only is increased virtual interaction and decreased real-life interaction a driver of anxiety, but it is also fundamentally tied to the development of Alzheimer's and dementia, eating disorders, substance abuse and addiction; all of which can only further increase the burden on society and on healthcare.

And this burden on society and healthcare will be much tougher to bear as we continue to make ourselves poorer.

Lockdown vs economy

Average of OECD estimate of weekly growth for four weeks to 6 March compared to same weeks last year. Stringency index averaged over same four weeks

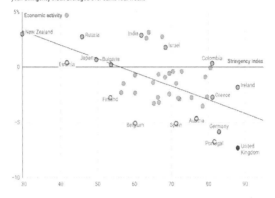

Economic downturn, as a result of the Lockdowns, of this magnitude means less funding for healthcare and social care; it means a driving up of inequality; and it means a greater number of earlier than was necessary deaths.

It also means less funding for our children's inalienable right to education at a time when one in six children will never catch-up on the education that has been denied to them over the past year.

And all of this is before we even consider the social costs: the division created in society that surpasses Brexit or anything that has been seen within the political spectrum; and the abhorrent retraction of civil liberties and freedoms of the individual that make life worth living.

In short, the costs are monumental.

In conclusion, the Lockdowns have failed to work in any way, and they lose on any cost-benefit analysis, with a significant margin for error on how much I may have underestimated their benefits.

There'll Be A Day

16th March 2021

Published in Lockdown Sceptics 17th March 2021

There'll be a day when we're together again,
A day when we laugh, smile, and hug our friends.
There'll be a day when we can all be free,
To think and speak, to believe and to be.
There'll be a day when our lives are our own,
To live as we please, and not be alone.
There'll be a day when we worry about dates,
About what to wear, and about being late.
There'll be a day when we've got things to do,
And when half the world doesn't fear the 'flu.
There'll be a day when we pack all the pubs,
Have a few pints and then head to the clubs.
There'll be a day when every single thing
That we've been denied comes back, beckoning
For one and all to just stand and sing
In one grand chorus as every note rings
Out.

Rings out and remembers that we're together;
Human beings, to each other tethered,
Connected by more than country or race,
Yet connected by just a smile on a face,
Connected by the desire to embrace,
Connected by our need for those days.

And those days are coming back with a kiss;
I promise you hugs, freedom, joy and bliss;
I promise you time with loved ones long-missed;
There'll be a day soon, I promise you this.

Closing Remarks and Thanks

19ᵗʰ March 2021

A while back, I decided that I would tie this book up after a year passed from the first piece, and it has now been a year since I started writing the articles, poems, and other pieces that have filled up this book.

A whole year.

I can quite clearly remember being sat in the pub with my brothers and mother on the Friday before the first Lockdown, but it simultaneously feels like a lot longer than a year ago.

I imagine time is bound to pass slower when one spends hours upon hours poring over "case" data, studies in medical journals, and Government legislation, all while being locked up in one's own home... But a year in which so much changed, in which so much was learnt, and in which there was so much struggle will also seem longer.

And this struggle wasn't simply with my mental health; I also regularly struggled with my position on the Lockdowns, with whether taking such an opposing view to the orthodoxy was worth it, and with the nagging questions such as, "if social interaction is reduced, then surely they must work?", or, "if I know all I know, why don't the Government and its advisors?", or, seeing as how the leaders of Florida and Sweden have appeared to have been aware of all the same information that I have been, "if the Government and its advisors do indeed know what I know, why aren't they changing tack?"

To answer the first, I return to the data. They're as conclusive as science gets, and certainly much more supportive of my position than of those who support the lockdowns.

To answer the second, I remind myself that at no point has a genuine cost-benefit analysis been performed by the Government, and that each group and subgroup of advisors has been tasked to deal with the spread of the SARS-CoV-2 virus and no other factor has been given its due attention. So, it is possible that they simply are not aware of either the lack of efficacy of the Lockdowns or the monumental harms they cause.

But, if they are aware, and I am in need of answering the third question, I remind myself that the Government is heavily invested in maintaining the narrative that it is their vaccine plan that sees us safely through this "pandemic"; I remind myself that those involved with perpetuating the Lockdowns stand to lose more than they'd gain in ending the Lockdowns; and I remind myself that so many other European countries are doing the same and that in ending the Lockdowns, the UK Government would be lifting their heads above the parapet.

What they seem to have failed to realise is that the longer they stay in the trenches, the deeper the hole they're digging for themselves becomes.

However, even with such surety in my position, I appreciate there is a small chance that I could be drastically wrong, about so much of this, and, in that eventuality, I will humble eat my words and seek to learn.

That said, seeing as how we're a year into this and I am yet to see a convincing argument against my position, I do believe that that *small chance* is in fact vanishingly small, and that is why I am happy to publish my thoughts and put my name to it.

I think, before I close, that it is worth saying that producing this book over the last year comes with an oddly bittersweet taste; while writing about all of this has been one of the few things that has kept me sane, and I am proud of the final product, there have been some truly dark days in the last twelve months. And although writing these pieces has been the primary thing that kept me going, I still wish that writing these pieces had never been necessary.

But they were necessary, there's no changing that now, and they did help me through.

And if I am to credit the writing of these pieces with keeping me going, then I will need to credit those who kept me writing with the very same, and on that note, I just want to say a few quick, and yet very important messages of thanks.

First up, and because I love a cliché, is my family. Marcus has an entire post named after him early on, in Part One, because of his constant and invaluable encouragement for me to keep writing, Susannah put to me exactly the sort of challenging questions that I needed, Edmund always offered an ear and gave me an opportunity to voice out my arguments – often over "a couple" of glasses of wine, Guy – as he partied out the later Lockdown days with his housemates in London – gave me a constant reminder of what it was we were fighting for, Alice was a regular sounding board and confidante, my mother was a source of strength, always available for a call, and my father provided the spark to start thinking for myself which ultimately led to my anti-lockdown position, and was also my editor for this book.

Next up, I have to offer a word of thanks to Ross. One of the most challenging aspects of the past year for me personally has been the near on relentless abandonment of friends; so, to have one stand by you throughout, read all of your pieces, always reply with something to the effect of, "another cracker", and, whether bored or not, to never have slipped away, or not replied to a message, put frankly, places him head and shoulders above many other friends.

There are a number of other messages of thanks I could offer up here, but the final one I am going to make goes to *Lockdown Sceptics*. I owe a huge debt of gratitude to Toby, Jonathan, Conor, Will, and the others not just for publishing a number of my pieces, but for the care they showed me, for the occasional late-night email chats, and, above all, for providing a sense of community in a time that would have been otherwise largely devoid of any such sense.

That may be it for the thanks, and that may be it for this book, but we are far from finished; the recovery job that is now needed needs each and every one of us to play our part – be that anything from completely changing one's career path through to helping your friend or neighbour in some small way with their current situation, however they've been affected by the lockdowns, and, just as importantly, regardless of how they've thought about the lockdowns.

Because this is the message I want to leave you with: whatever has happened throughout the past twelve months, we are still human beings, and we still rely on and need each other; now is not the time for retribution against our compatriots, and certainly not against those who succumbed to the constant fear-inducing messages of the Government and Mainstream Media.

Now is the time to forgive and be there for whoever it is who might need you. Now is the time to repair relationships, and to repair this torn and divided nation to what we all know it can be and should be.

The End

Printed in Great Britain
by Amazon

58866711R00151